JAMESTOWN  EDUCATION

SIGNATURE READING

LEVEL H

 **Glencoe**

New York, New York   Columbus, Ohio   Chicago, Illinois   Peoria, Illinois   Woodland Hills, California

JAMESTOWN EDUCATION

Reviewers

Marsha Miller, Ed.D
Reading Specialist
Elgin High School
1200 Maroon Drive
Elgin, IL 60120

Kati Pearson
Orange County Public Schools
Literacy Coordinator
Carver Middle School
4500 West Columbia Street
Orlando, FL 32811

Lynda Pearson
Assistant Principal
Reading Specialist
Lied Middle School
5350 Tropical Parkway
Las Vegas, NV 89130

Suzanne Zweig
Reading Specialist/Consultant
Sullivan High School
6631 N. Bosworth
Chicago, IL 60626

Cover Image: Donald E. Carroll/Getty Images

Mc Graw Hill **Glencoe**

The **McGraw·Hill** Companies

Send all queries to:
Glencoe/McGraw-Hill
8787 Orion Place
Columbus, OH 43240-4027

ACC Library Services
Austin, Texas

1 2 3 4 5 6 7 8 9 045 09 08 07 06

Contents

How to Use This Book

Working Through the Lessons

The following descriptions will help you work your way through the lessons in this book.

Building Background will help you get ready to read. In this section you might begin a chart, discuss a question, or learn more about the topic of the selection.

Vocabulary Builder will help you start thinking about—and using—the selection vocabulary. You might draw a diagram and label it with vocabulary words, make a word map, match vocabulary words to their synonyms or antonyms, or use the words to predict what might happen in the selection.

Strategy Builder will introduce you to the strategy that you will use to read the selection. First you will read a definition of the strategy. Then you will see an example of how to use it. Often, you will be given ways to better organize or visualize what you will be reading.

Strategy Break will appear within the reading selection. It will show you how to apply the strategy you just learned to the first part of the selection.

Strategy Follow-up will ask you to apply the same strategy to the second part of the selection. Most of the time, you will work on your own to complete this section. Sometimes, however, you might work with a partner or a group of classmates.

Personal Checklist questions will ask you to rate how well you did in the lesson. When you finish totaling your score, you will enter it on the graphs on page 209.

Vocabulary Check will follow up on the work you did in the Vocabulary Builder. After you total your score, you will enter it on page 209.

Strategy Check will follow up on the strategy work that you did in the lesson. After you total your score, you will enter it on page 209.

Comprehension Check will check your understanding of the selection. After you total your score, you will enter it on page 209.

Extending will give ideas for activities that are related to the selection. Some activities will help you learn more about the topic of the selection. Others might ask you to respond to the selection by dramatizing, writing, or drawing something.

Resources such as books, recordings, videos, and Web sites will help you complete the Extending activities.

Graphing Your Progress

The information and graphs on pages 208–209 will help you track your progress as you work through this book. **Graph 1** will help you record your scores for the Personal Checklist and the Vocabulary, Strategy, and Comprehension Checks. **Graph 2** will help you track your overall progress across the book. You'll be able to see your areas of strength, as well as any areas that could use improvement. You and your teacher can discuss ways to work on those areas.

A Mare Called Lucky

corral

coulee

foals

gelding

loft

mare

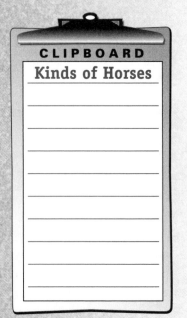

CLIPBOARD

Kinds of Horses

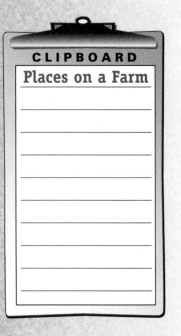

CLIPBOARD

Places on a Farm

Building Background

In the story you are about to read, Jessie's dad likes to make "corny" jokes. We all know people who make silly jokes or say one thing when they mean something else. Sometimes what they say makes us laugh, but at other times it hurts our feelings or makes us angry or causes misunderstandings. Can you think of a time when that happened to you?

Jessie and her parents live on a farm and raise cattle. They need healthy horses to help them with the work. But when Jessie falls in love with a new mare with a problem, the family faces some serious decisions. By yourself or with a partner, predict what those decisions might be.

Vocabulary Builder

1. Sometimes when you read a selection, you find words that are related to each other and to a particular topic. It's important to understand those words, or the selection may not make sense to you.

2. Before you begin reading "A Mare Called Lucky" read the vocabulary words in the margin. Then write any of the words that you already know on the appropriate clipboards.

3. Later, as you read the story, find the rest of the boldfaced vocabulary words and use context to try to figure out what they mean. If context doesn't help, find the words in a dictionary. Then write the words on the appropriate clipboards.

4. Save your work. You will use it again in the Vocabulary Check.

Strategy Builder

Making Predictions While Reading a Story

- When you read a story, you often make predictions. A **prediction** is a kind of guess that you make based on information or clues that the author provides. Those clues are called **context clues**. They "set the scene" and help you understand what's happening. They also help you predict what might happen next.

- As you read "A Mare Called Lucky" you will pause twice to make predictions. At Strategy Break #1, you will write down your predictions. You also will write which clues helped you make your predictions.

- At Strategy Break #2, you will check your earlier predictions. Then you will make more predictions, and you will tell which clues helped you make them.

- After you finish reading the story, you will see if any of your predictions matched what happened in the story.

A Mare Called Lucky

by H. J. Hutchins

See if you can use clues that the author provides to help you make predictions while you read.

"I think I just bought a blind horse."

Jessie sat on the mare's warm, sleek back and watched her dad slowly wave his cowboy hat before the horse's eyes. At first she thought it was one of his corny jokes. When he'd called her out to the **corral** a half hour ago, he'd said there was a giant gopher in there—the strangest-looking animal he'd ever seen.

Well, there had been an animal in the corral, all right, but not a giant gopher. It was a horse, a lovely **mare**. She was far younger than Blackie, the ancient, stubborn **gelding** Jessie normally rode, but not as headstrong as her dad's cattle horse, Windego. Jessie had fallen in love with this perfect buckskin mare in about two seconds flat.

"It's not a gopher?" her dad had asked in mock amazement. "But it's the right color—that nice, tawny brown."

Sometimes her dad's corny lines drove Jessie crazy. And now he was saying this perfect mare couldn't see. It had to be another one of his jokes . . . but it wasn't very funny.

"This mare is blind. She won't go any faster than a walk because she's scared to."

Jessie's dad stepped back, shaking his head in dismay at his horse-trading abilities.

Jessie still didn't want to believe it. She urged the mare forward again, clucking her tongue and nudging the sleek, light-brown sides with her heels. "Hee-ya!" she yelled, hoping against hope that the horse would spring forward. But she didn't. Jessie slid off the mare's back and walked to her head. She passed her hand before the clear brown eyes. Her dad was right. The most perfect mare in the world couldn't see.

After supper, Jessie and her mom went out to the corral and took the mare a bucket of oats. Jessie's dad was talking on the phone. He soon came out to join them.

"Sanders says he didn't know the mare was blind," he said.

"The man you bought her from?" asked Jessie's mom. "How could he not have known?"

"She was with some other horses at a sale last spring," said Jessie's dad. "He wanted the other horses, so he took her, too. He didn't pay much attention to her because she was young. He turned her out into his far pasture for the winter. When he brought her up with the others last week, she was so gentle, he decided to sell her without training her. He says if I take her down and sell her as horse meat, he'll give me my money back."

Horse meat, thought Jessie. The most perfect mare in the world killed for horse meat!

"No," said Jessie quickly. "It's O.K. I can ride Blackie for lots more years. We can keep this mare to have **foals**."

Jessie's dad shook his head. "I phoned the vet," he said. "The blindness could be hereditary—that means her foals could be born blind as well. We can't keep a blind mare that has blind foals. We don't have enough pasture. Everything on this farm has to pay its way—either by producing something we can sell or by helping out with the work. It's the only way we can keep the farm going."

"That's true, Jessie," said her mother sadly. "We can keep Blackie because he's already worked hard for us, but any new horse we get must be able to work cattle or have foals that can learn."

"But do you know for sure her foals will be blind?" Jessie pressed. "Couldn't something have happened to make her blind?"

"She might have had a bad infection—that would mean she'd still have healthy foals," Jessie's dad admitted. "But her eyes look normal, so there's no way of telling."

"Couldn't we at least try and see?" asked Jessie.

Her dad looked hard at Jessie from beneath the rim of his cowboy hat.

"If we let her have a foal and it's born blind, I'll have to sell them both as horse meat for very little money. Both of them, Jessie. It might be easier just to take the mare away now."

Jessie looked at the mare's blind, trusting eyes. "She deserves a chance," Jessie said.

Her dad glanced at Jessie's mom and then turned back to Jessie.

 Stop here for Strategy Break #1.

Strategy Break #1

1. What do you predict will happen next? _____

_____

2. Why do you think so? _____

_____

3. What clues from the story helped you make your prediction(s)? _____

_____

_____

 Go on reading to see what happens.

"All right," he said. "So long as you understand what might have to be done, we'll give her that chance."

Jessie wrapped her arms around the mare's warm neck. "We'll call her Lucky," she said.

That summer, Jessie and Lucky became friends. Jessie didn't care that she couldn't ride Lucky a million miles an hour up and down the **coulee**, as she had always dreamed of riding her own horse. Sometimes she just rode at a walk around the pasture. Sometimes she braided Lucky's mane and tail and curried her to a gloss. Sometimes Jessie just lay on Lucky's broad back and watched hawks soar while Lucky grazed.

When cold weather came, Jessie herself took Lucky out to the far pasture to winter with Blackie and Windego. She was afraid the two bigger horses might pick on the mare, but the opposite happened. When Lucky wandered away from the other two, she would raise her head and nicker, and Blackie and Windego would whinny back until she found them again. During the long evenings, Jessie's dad noticed that Lucky sometimes roamed around the field as if she could see—or at least felt more at home—in the darkness. On weekends Jessie took oats out to her and buried her hands in Lucky's thick winter coat. And as spring crept onto the prairie, Lucky's belly widened with the foal she was carrying.

"I can't see Lucky anywhere, Mom," said Jessie from the shed roof early one spring morning.

"She's just hidden by Blackie," said her mother, coming out of the house with Jessie's jacket and books. "Quick. The school bus has turned the corner."

Jessie grabbed her jacket and books and raced for the bus. As it drove along the pasture, she searched for Lucky but couldn't find her. Jessie was sure of it now: the mare had sought some secret, sheltered spot to have her foal.

School took forever that day. When Jessie returned home on the bus, there was still no buckskin mare in the far pasture. There was no mare in the pasture by the house, either. As she walked up the lane, Jessie saw her dad waiting by the gate. There was something about the way he stood there that she didn't like.

 Stop here for Strategy Break #2.

Strategy Break #2

1. Do your earlier predictions match what happened? _____ Why or why not? _____
   _____

2. What do you predict will happen next? _____
   _____
   _____

3. Why do you think so? _____
   _____

4. What clues from the story helped you make your prediction(s)? _____
   _____
   _____

 Go on reading to see what happens.

I don't want to talk to him, she thought. I know what's happened. The foal is blind, and he's taken both of them away. Now he's going to explain why he had to. I hate adults. I hate explanations. It's not right. It's not fair.

Jessie bolted past her dad and the house. She scrambled behind the out-buildings and climbed her secret way into the barn **loft**. She buried herself in the safe half-darkness of hay where only narrow shards of sunlight squeezed through the boards. Hiding. Hiding.

"Jessie! Jessie!" Her dad was calling from the barn doorway. How did he know where she was? Why couldn't he just let her be?

"I wanted to tell you—I went into town and bought Lucky a Seeing Eye dog this morning."

Another of his jokes, though Jessie. Another of his corny . . .

She stopped in midthought. Her dad made corny jokes, but he never made cruel ones. Then she heard a heavy movement and a low nicker in one of the stalls below her. She crawled to an opening and peered down. Below her stood Lucky and the new foal—a beautiful foal, all legs and bones and wobbles. Jessie dropped a handful of hay through the opening. The foal's head bobbed comically as its eyes caught the movement. It could see!

"I thought Lucky might feel more reassured in the protection of the barn," her dad said. "I brought her in last night."

Jessie knew then that her father had been every bit as worried as she. He must have come in from the fields this afternoon just so he could share the good news with her. In her own fear, she'd forgotten how much her dad loved horses of all kinds—even blind horses. He probably loved horses as much as he loved his own corny jokes.

Jessie climbed down into the warmth and life below her. She didn't know what to say. No, that wasn't true—she knew exactly what to say. "Seeing Eye dog indeed," Jessie scoffed. "I suppose we'll have to name it Rover."

"Not a bad idea," said her dad as the foal's bright eyes fixed on Jessie's outstretched hand and it arched its neck forward to nuzzle her fingers. "Not a bad idea at all." ●

Strategy Follow-up

Go back and look at the predictions that you wrote in this lesson. Do any of them match what actually happened in this story? Why or why not?_____

_____

_____

_____

_____

_____

_____

✓ Personal Checklist

Read each question and put a check (✓) in the correct box.

1. How well do you understand what happened in "A Mare Called Lucky"?
   - ☐ 3 (extremely well)
   - ☐ 2 (fairly well)
   - ☐ 1 (not well)

2. In Building Background, how well were you able to predict what decisions the family would make?
   - ☐ 3 (extremely well)
   - ☐ 2 (fairly well)
   - ☐ 1 (not well)

3. By the time you finished this story, how many vocabulary words were you able to write on the appropriate clipboards?
   - ☐ 3 (5–6 words)
   - ☐ 2 (3–4 words)
   - ☐ 1 (0–2 words)

4. How well were you able to use context clues to predict what would happen next in this story?
   - ☐ 3 (extremely well)
   - ☐ 2 (fairly well)
   - ☐ 1 (not well)

5. How well do you understand why Jessie's dad made the joke about the Seeing Eye dog?
   - ☐ 3 (extremely well)
   - ☐ 2 (fairly well)
   - ☐ 1 (not well)

Vocabulary Check

Look back at the work you did in the Vocabulary Builder. Then answer each question by circling the correct letter.

1. When horses are brought in from the range, where are they kept?
   - a. in a corral
   - b. in a loft
   - c. in a coulee

2. What is a neutered male horse called?
   - a. a foal
   - b. a gelding
   - c. a mare

3. Which phrase best describes a coulee?
   - a. a large, flat prairie
   - b. a deep ravine or valley
   - c. the upper room in a barn

4. What is a mother horse called?
   - a. a foal
   - b. a gelding
   - c. a mare

5. What are newborn horses called?
   - a. foals
   - b. geldings
   - c. mares

Add the numbers that you just checked to get your total score. (For example, if you checked 3, 2, 3, 2, and 1, your total score would be 11.) Fill in your score here. Then turn to page 209 and transfer your score onto Graph 1.

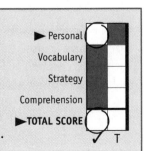

Check your answers with your teacher. Give yourself 1 point for each correct answer, and fill in your Vocabulary score here. Then turn to page 209 and transfer your score onto Graph 1.

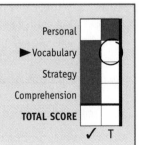

Strategy Check

Look back at what you wrote at each Strategy Break. Then answer these questions:

1. If you had predicted that Jessie's dad would sell the mare, which clue would have best supported your prediction?

    a. "We can't keep a mare that has blind foals."

    b. "But her eyes look normal, so there's no way of telling."

    c. "Couldn't we at least try and see?"

2. If you had predicted that Jessie would be able to keep the mare, which clue would have best supported your prediction?

    a. "He says if I take her down and sell her as horse meat, he'll give me my money back."

    b. "She might have had a bad infection—that would mean she'd still have healthy foals."

    c. "Everything on this farm has to pay its way."

3. At Strategy Break #2, which prediction would have best fit the story?

    a. Jessie's dad is going to tell her he sold Lucky.

    b. Lucky is out hiding somewhere in the pasture.

    c. Lucky has not had her foal yet.

4. If you had predicted that the foal would be blind, which clue would have best supported your prediction?

    a. "I can't see Lucky anywhere, Mom," said Jessie.

    b. Jessie was sure of it now: the mare had sought some secret, sheltered spot to have her foal.

    c. There was something about the way he stood there that she didn't like.

5. What might the title of this story have helped you predict?

    a. the mare would have a blind foal

    b. the mare would have a foal that could see

    c. the mare would be sold as horse meat

Comprehension Check

Review the story if necessary. Then answer these questions:

1. What does Jessie's dad learn about the mare after he brings her home?

    a. that she is a large gopher

    b. that she can't see

    c. that she won't let Jessie ride her

2. Why does Jessie's dad think he should sell the mare as horse meat?

    a. The previous owner had tricked him into buying a blind mare.

    b. The mare is too small to work on a farm.

    c. The mare's blindness might be hereditary.

3. Why do you think Jessie might have named the mare Lucky?

    a. because the mare is lucky to get a Seeing Eye dog

    b. because she hopes the name will bring the mare good luck

    c. because she is lucky to have the mare for a pet

4. What does Jessie's dad mean when he says he bought Lucky a Seeing Eye dog?

    a. He bought a dog named Rover for Jessie.

    b. He bought a dog to help with farm chores.

    c. He's making a joke about Lucky's new foal.

5. At the end of this story, what does Jessie's family decide to do with Lucky?

    a. They decide to keep her and let her have foals.

    b. They decide to sell her as horse meat.

    c. They decide to keep her as a friend for Jessie.

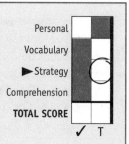

Check your answers with your teacher. Give yourself 1 point for each correct answer, and fill in your Strategy score here. Then turn to page 209 and transfer your score onto Graph 1.

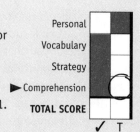

Check your answers with your teacher. Give yourself 1 point for each correct answer, and fill in your Comprehension score here. Then turn to page 209 and transfer your score onto Graph 1.

Extending

Choose one or more of these activities:

WRITE CHAPTER TWO
Imagine that "A Mare Called Lucky" is the first chapter in a book about the adventures of Jessie and her family. Predict what might happen next as Lucky's foal begins to grow up. Use information from this story and the resources listed below to help you write the second chapter.

TAKE NOTE OF WHAT PEOPLE SAY
In "A Mare Called Lucky" Jessie's father likes to tell corny jokes. Listen to how your classmates, friends, and family use language. Collect examples of silly jokes or things that people say when they really mean something else.

FIND OUT ABOUT ANIMAL HEALTH
Find out more about the illnesses and diseases of horses or other animals. Log on to the Internet, or go to the library to get more information. Then design a poster that shows what you've learned.

Resources

Books
Betancourt, Jeanne. *The Blind Pony.* Turtleback Books, 2001.

Henry, Marguerite. *Album of Horses.* Aladdin, 1993.

Isenbart, Hans-Heinrich, and Thomas David (photographer). *Birth of a Foal.* Carolrhoda Nature Watch Books. Carolrhoda, 1986.

Rounds, Glen. *The Blind Colt.* Holiday House, 1989.

Web Site
http://www.vetmed.ucdavis.edu/ceh/htips.html
This Web site provides tips relating to horse health.

LESSON 2 The Parcel Post Kid

Building Background

The selection you are about to read is nonfiction. **Nonfiction** is based on facts, true events, and real people. We often read nonfiction because we are curious and want to learn more about a topic. Sometimes we read nonfiction because we need to know how to do or make something. Think about all the nonfiction that you have read in the last week. List as many kinds as you can remember on a separate sheet of paper.

"The Parcel Post Kid" is a nonfiction account of something that really happened in 1914. It describes the unique way in which a young girl was sent to visit her grandmother when her parents couldn't afford the train fare.

flabbergasted

parcel post

postmaster

Vocabulary Builder

1. The words in the margin are from "The Parcel Post Kid." Before you read the selection, read the following pairs of sentences. One of the sentences in each pair uses the boldfaced vocabulary word correctly, and one uses it incorrectly. Put a check ✓ in front of each sentence that uses the word correctly. If you are unsure of a word, guess for now. Then after you've read the selection, change your answers if necessary.

_____ a. Our grandfather sent us a box of books by **parcel post**.

_____ b. Stacks of **parcel post** were used to build a sturdy fence.

_____ a. The job of the **postmaster** is to serve food to the customers.

_____ b. The job of the **postmaster** is to run the post office.

_____ a. Carlos was **flabbergasted** when he learned that he had won a million dollars.

_____ b. Hard work and a lack of sleep **flabbergasted** Shauna so much that she fell asleep.

2. Save your work. You will use it again in the Vocabulary Check.

Strategy Builder

Following Sequence While You Read

- "The Parcel Post Kid" describes a series of events in the order in which they happened. That order—and the organizational pattern of this selection—is called **sequence**.

- To make the sequence of events as clear as possible, authors often use **signal words**. Examples of signal words include *first, next, all at once, after a while,* and *early that morning.*

- Read the paragraph below. Notice how the signal words help you follow the sequence of events.

> <u>From the very start</u>, Mitch's first day of school was a disaster. <u>To begin with</u>, he didn't hear his alarm, so he woke up late. That meant he didn't have time for a shower. <u>Next</u> he burned his breakfast. <u>Then</u> he jumped onto his bike only to discover that it had a flat tire. That meant that Mitch had to walk to school. He walked and ran as fast as he could. <u>Just before he got to school</u>, he dropped all his books. His heart began to race, and his face turned red. <u>Suddenly</u> Mitch awoke with a start. He realized it was Saturday, and he had been dreaming!

If you wanted to track the main events in the paragraph above, you could organize them on a **sequence chain**. It would look like this:

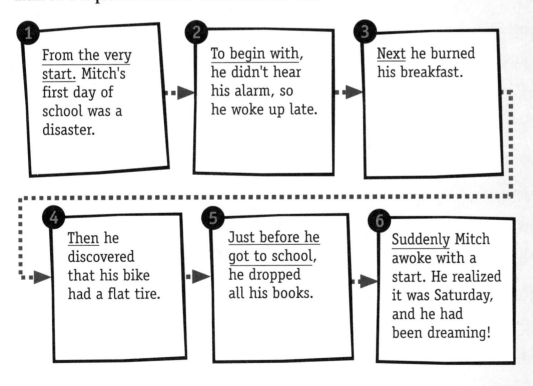

1. <u>From the very start.</u> Mitch's first day of school was a disaster.

2. <u>To begin with,</u> he didn't hear his alarm, so he woke up late.

3. <u>Next</u> he burned his breakfast.

4. <u>Then</u> he discovered that his bike had a flat tire.

5. <u>Just before he got to school,</u> he dropped all his books.

6. Suddenly Mitch awoke with a start. He realized it was Saturday, and he had been dreaming!

The Parcel Post Kid

by Michael O. Tunnell

As you read the first part of this selection, apply the strategies that you just learned. Notice the underlined signal words. They will give you a more exact picture of when things happened.

On a cold February morning in 1914, Leonard Mochel arrived for work. He was a railroad postal clerk and rode in the mail car that traveled between Grangeville and Lewiston, Idaho. But on this particular morning, he had more than his lunch with him. Accompanying him was his five-year-old cousin, Charlotte May Pierstorff.

When the **postmaster** saw May and her small traveling bag, he thought that Leonard was going to buy her a train ticket. Imagine his surprise when Leonard announced that he wanted to *mail* May to her grandmother in Lewiston!

May's train fare would have cost $1.55, a lot of money in those days. But May's parents had discovered that she could be mailed for only 53¢— if the post office would accept May as a package. Leonard thought it was a crazy idea, but he agreed to try.

We would never think of mailing a human being today, but things were different in 1914. For one thing, sending heavy packages by mail was something new, so who could guess what might be allowed? And in 1914, mail was carried in rolling post offices instead of in the bellies of airplanes or the backs of trucks. Postal clerks like Leonard Mochel would sort mail while trains traveled between towns. If May were mailed, she would have her cousin Leonard's company as well as a safe and comfortable place to ride.

When the postmaster checked his book of rules, he found several things that he could not mail. No poisons. No insects. No reptiles. Nothing that smelled strongly. According to Leonard, the postmaster had a few funny things to say that morning. Maybe he sniffed May, laughed, and declared that she passed the smell test.

Live animals were also forbidden, but the postmaster found that it was all right to send baby chicks by **parcel post**. So he classified May as a baby chick, weighed her in at 48 1/2 pounds (which may have included her small suitcase), and attached 53¢ in postage to her bag. As well as being "stamped," May was also "addressed":

Deliver to Mrs. C. G. Vennigerholz

1156 Twelfth Avenue

Lewiston, Idaho

Leonard helped May into the mail car, and at 7:00 A.M., the train chugged out of the station.

 Stop here for the Strategy Break.

Strategy Break

If you were to create a sequence chain to show the most important events in this section so far, it might look like the one below. Notice the underlined signal words.

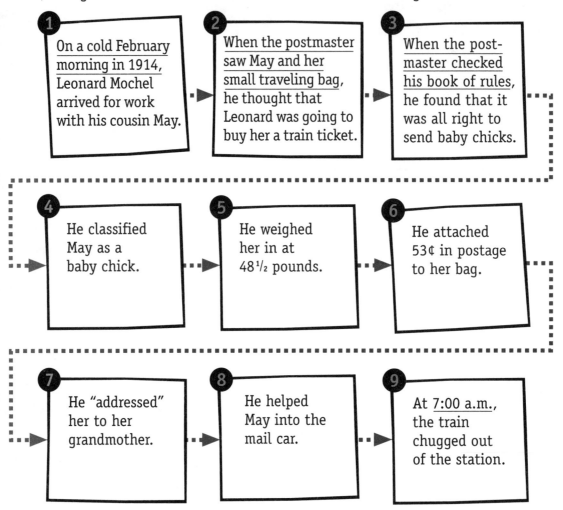

1 On <u>a cold February morning in 1914</u>, Leonard Mochel arrived for work with his cousin May.

2 <u>When the postmaster saw May and her small traveling bag</u>, he thought that Leonard was going to buy her a train ticket.

3 <u>When the postmaster checked his book of rules</u>, he found that it was all right to send baby chicks.

4 He classified May as a baby chick.

5 He weighed her in at 48½ pounds.

6 He attached 53¢ in postage to her bag.

7 He "addressed" her to her grandmother.

8 He helped May into the mail car.

9 At <u>7:00 a.m.</u>, the train chugged out of the station.

As you continue reading, keep paying attention to the sequence of events. Also keep looking for signal words. At the end of the selection, you will use some of them to complete a sequence chain of your own.

Go on reading.

Thus began the winding, seventy-seven-mile trip through the mountains to Lewiston. The train crawled through dark tunnels and over tall wooden trestles that stretched across the deep canyons. As it jolted and swayed over the tracks, May began to get dizzy. She hurried to the door to get some fresh air. Immediately Harry Morris, the conductor, spotted her and demanded to see May's ticket. When Leonard explained that May was actually a parcel and showed him the 53¢ in stamps, Mr. Morris laughed. "I've seen everything now!" he said. He was certain May's adventure would make a terrific story for the newspapers.

Traveling about nineteen miles an hour, the train finally reached Lewiston at 11:00 A.M. Leonard turned the Lewiston mail—including May—over to a clerk in the post office. Then he promptly "received" May from the clerk and delivered her to her grandmother. Grandma Mary was **flabbergasted** when May appeared on her doorstep. No one had told her that her granddaughter was coming to visit, and delivery by mail was an extra shock!

Meanwhile, Harry Morris wasted no time in reporting May's adventure to the newspaper. The *Gem State Banner* printed a story with the headline "Send Girl Aged 4 by Parcel Post." Even though the paper got May's age wrong, it managed to stir up trouble.

Two days later, another headline appeared in a paper from nearby Spokane, Washington: "Illegal to Send Child by Mail." Post office inspectors had gotten wind of May's story, and Leonard's job was on the line. The rule banning live animals from the mail excludes children, too, said the inspectors. And because May had been mailed, people were now asking to mail other live animals. Why, one man wanted to send his dog to Spokane!

In the end, Leonard kept his job, partly because May's parents agreed to pay half the train fare. But never again was anyone mailed by parcel post. ●

Strategy Follow-up

Now complete this sequence chain for the second part of "The Parcel Post Kid." Underline any signal words that you use. Some of the chain has been filled in for you.

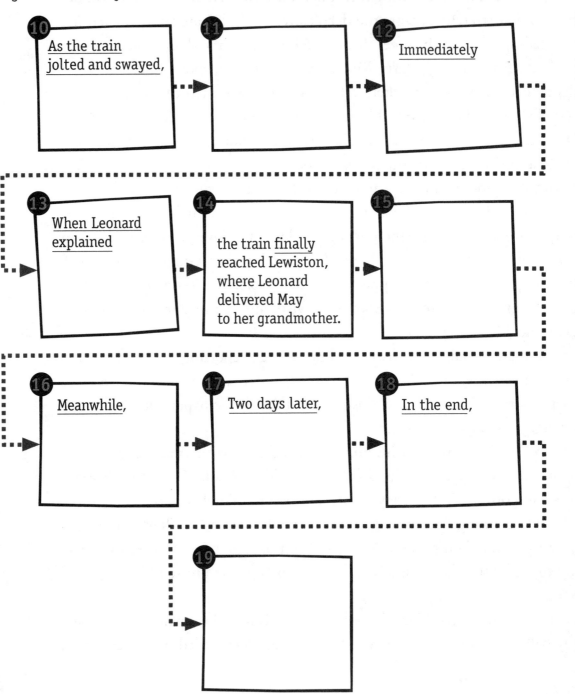

10 <u>As the train jolted and swayed,</u>

11

12 Immediately

13 <u>When Leonard explained</u>

14 the train <u>finally</u> reached Lewiston, where Leonard delivered May to her grandmother.

15

16 <u>Meanwhile,</u>

17 <u>Two days later,</u>

18 <u>In the end,</u>

19

✓ Personal Checklist

Read each question and put a check (✓) in the correct box.

1. How well were you able to use the information in Building Background to help you understand nonfiction?
   - ☐ 3 (extremely well)
   - ☐ 2 (fairly well)
   - ☐ 1 (not well)

2. By the time you finished this selection, how many words were you able to identify as being used correctly in sentences?
   - ☐ 3 (3 words)
   - ☐ 2 (2 words)
   - ☐ 1 (0–1 word)

3. How well were you able to complete the sequence chain in the Strategy Follow-up?
   - ☐ 3 (extremely well)
   - ☐ 2 (fairly well)
   - ☐ 1 (not well)

4. How well do you understand why May was mailed to her grandmother?
   - ☐ 3 (extremely well)
   - ☐ 2 (fairly well)
   - ☐ 1 (not well)

5. At the end of this selection, how well do you understand why Leonard's job was on the line?
   - ☐ 3 (extremely well)
   - ☐ 2 (fairly well)
   - ☐ 1 (not well)

Vocabulary Check

Look back at the work you did in the Vocabulary Builder. Then answer each question by circling the correct letter.

1. In which sentence is *parcel post* used correctly?
   a. Kara sent the gifts parcel post to get them to Avery for his birthday.
   b. George wanted to send the letter full post rather than parcel post.
   c. Henry dug parcel post after parcel post as he built the fence around the yard.

2. In which sentence is *postmaster* used correctly?
   a. As postmaster, David delivered all the mail in his town.
   b. As postmaster, Marsha was in charge of the local post office.
   c. The postmaster governed the town with fairness and honesty.

3. In which sentence is *flabbergasted* used correctly?
   a. When he couldn't figure out the math problem, Matt became flabbergasted.
   b. When everyone yelled, "Surprise!" Barbara was too flabbergasted to speak.
   c. After competing in the marathon, Jack felt hungry and flabbergasted.

4. Which meaning of *post* fits the context of this selection?
   a. place where a soldier is stationed
   b. piece of wood or metal used as a support
   c. system of sending packages by mail

5. Which word is a synonym for *flabbergasted*?
   a. shocked
   b. flabby
   c. tired

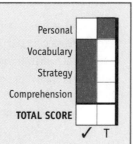

Add the numbers that you just checked to get your Personal Checklist score. Fill in your score here. Then turn to page 209 and transfer your score onto Graph 1.

Personal
Vocabulary
Strategy
Comprehension
TOTAL SCORE
✓ T

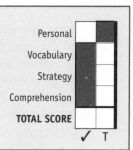

Check your answers with your teacher. Give yourself 1 point for each correct answer, and fill in your Vocabulary score here. Then turn to page 209 and transfer your score onto Graph 1.

Personal
Vocabulary
Strategy
Comprehension
TOTAL SCORE
✓ T

Strategy Check

Review the sequence chain that you completed in the Strategy Follow-up. Then answer these questions:

1. What happened as the train jolted and swayed?
   a. May began to get dizzy.
   b. Leonard explained that May was a parcel.
   c. A headline appeared in the newspaper.

2. Which of the following is *not* an example of signal words?
   a. two days later
   b. imagine his surprise
   c. in the end

3. Which signal word means "at the same time"?
   a. never
   b. finally
   c. meanwhile

4. While May was being delivered to her grandmother, what else was happening?
   a. The conductor was demanding to see May's ticket.
   b. Harry Morris was reporting May's adventure to the newspaper.
   c. Leonard was telling the conductor that May was a parcel.

5. What might you have written for event 19?
   a. <u>Never again</u> was anyone mailed by parcel post.
   b. <u>Meanwhile</u>, Harry Morris reported May's adventure to the newspaper.
   c. <u>Immediately</u>, the conductor demanded to see May's ticket.

Comprehension Check

Review the selection if necessary. Then answer these questions:

1. Why did May's parents mail her to her grandmother?
   a. They wanted her to travel with her cousin.
   b. They couldn't afford her train fare.
   c. They thought she'd get there faster.

2. In what part of the train did May ride?
   a. in a passenger car
   b. in the caboose
   c. in the mail car

3. How was the postmaster able to approve May's trip?
   a. He said she was too young to travel as an adult.
   b. He classified her as a baby chick.
   c. He said she was traveling with her cousin.

4. How long did it take the train to get from Grangeville to Lewiston?
   a. 4 hours
   b. 8 hours
   c. 12 hours

5. Why did May's cousin almost lose his job?
   a. Many people felt that what he did was illegal.
   b. His actions caused a lot of people to try to mail animals.
   c. Both of the above answers are correct.

Check your answers with your teacher. Give yourself 1 point for each correct answer, and fill in your Strategy score here. Then turn to page 209 and transfer your score onto Graph 1.

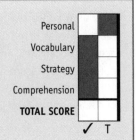

Check your answers with your teacher. Give yourself 1 point for each correct answer, and fill in your Comprehension score here. Then turn to page 209 and transfer your score onto Graph 1.

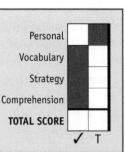

Extending

Choose one or more of these activities:

COMPARE AND CONTRAST

Get a copy of Michael O. Tunnell's book *Mailing May*, which is listed in the resources on this page. Compare and contrast the book with the article you just read. In your opinion, which version tells the story more effectively? Why? Which version did you enjoy more? Why?

RESEARCH RAILROAD HISTORY

With a partner, research railroad travel in the early part of the 20th century. Create a mural and/or a time line to show what it was like.

WRITE A JOURNAL ENTRY

Imagine that your are May or her cousin Leonard. Write a journal entry describing the trip from your point of view. Use the sequence chains in this lesson to help you track the sequence of events.

Resources

Book

Tunnell, Michael O. *Mailing May.* HarperCollins Juvenile Books, 2000.

Web Site

http://sdrm.org/history/timeline/
This Web site presents a time line of the development of the railroad in the United States and Britain.

Mother and Daughter

Building Background

Sometimes telling a good story is like being a sportscaster announcing what the players are doing during a game. The "announcer" in the case of a fictional story is called the narrator. The **narrator** tells what is happening in the story. When the narrator is not actually a character in the story, we say that he or she is telling the story from the **third-person point of view**. In the story you are about to read, a third-person narrator observes the relationship between a mother and daughter and tells readers what these characters say, do, think, and feel.

chile verde

"Las Mañanitas"

Mamacita

m'ija

tienes que estudiar mucho

Vocabulary Builder

1. All of the words in the margin are Spanish words used by Mexican Americans in the United States. The words are in *italics* because they are not part of the English language and are considered foreign words.

2. Before you read "Mother and Daughter" try to match the words in Column 1 to their definitions in Column 2. If you are unsure of any of the words, guess for now. Then after you've read the selection, change your answers if necessary.

3. Save your work. You will use it again in the Vocabulary Check.

COLUMN 1	COLUMN 2
chile verde	a Mexican birthday song
"Las Mañanitas"	you have to study a lot
Mamacita	little mama
m'ija	a stew-like dish
tienes que estudiar mucho	my daughter

Strategy Builder

Drawing Conclusions About Characters

- A **conclusion** is a decision that you reach after thinking about certain facts or information. When you read a story, you often draw conclusions based on information that the author gives you about the characters, the setting, or particular events.

- You can draw conclusions about the **characters** in a story by paying attention to their words, thoughts, feelings, and actions. These character **traits**, or qualities, help you understand the characters better. They also help you understand why the characters do what they do.

- Read the following description of a character named Grace. Then look at the **character map** below the description. It shows the conclusions that one student drew about Grace—and why.

Ben's little sister Grace is always trying to go everywhere with him. If he asks her not to go, she will follow him anyway. Grace also spies on Ben and his friends. She makes up songs about what Ben and his friends do. And then she teases him by singing them over and over. But worst of all, Grace always tells their parents everything that Ben and his friends are doing. If she doesn't know anything that will get Ben into trouble, she makes something up.

CHARACTER TRAIT:
tag along
Example:
She always follows Ben around, even when he asks her not to.

CHARACTER TRAIT:
nosy
Example:
She spies on Ben and his friends and then makes up songs about what they do.

Character: GRACE

CHARACTER TRAIT:
tattletale
Example:
She tells their parents everything that Ben and his friends are doing.

CHARACTER TRAIT:
troublemaker
Example:
If she doesn't know anything that will get Ben into trouble, she makes something up.

Mother and Daughter

by Gary Soto

As you read this story, you will meet two interesting characters—Mrs. Moreno and her daughter Yollie. Look for clues that the author provides to help you draw conclusions about each character.

Yollie's mother, Mrs. Moreno, was a large woman who wore a muumuu and butterfly-shaped glasses. She liked to water her lawn in the evening and wave at low-riders, who would stare at her behind their smoky sunglasses and laugh. Now and then a low-rider from Belmont Avenue would make his car jump and shout *"Mamacita!"* But most of the time they just stared and wondered how she got so large.

Mrs. Moreno had a strange sense of humor. Once, Yollie and her mother were watching a late-night movie called "They Came to Look." It was about creatures from the underworld who had climbed through molten lava to walk the earth. But Yollie, who had played soccer all day with the kids next door, was too tired to be scared. Her eyes closed but sprang open when her mother screamed, "Look, Yollie! Oh, you missed a scary part. The guy's face was all ugly!"

But Yollie couldn't keep her eyes open. They fell shut again and stayed shut, even when her mother screamed and slammed a heavy palm on the arm of her chair.

"Mom, wake me up when the movie's over so I can go to bed," mumbled Yollie.

"OK, Yollie, I wake you," said her mother through a mouthful of popcorn.

But after the movie ended, instead of waking her daughter, Mrs. Moreno laughed under her breath, turned the TV and lights off, and tiptoed to bed. Yollie woke up in the middle of the night and didn't know where she was. For a moment she thought she was dead. Maybe something from the underworld had lifted her from her house and carried her into the earth's belly. She blinked her sleepy eyes, looked around at the darkness, and called, "Mom? Mom, where are you?" But there was no answer, just the throbbing hum of the refrigerator.

Finally, Yollie's grogginess cleared and she realized her mother had gone to bed, leaving her on the couch. Another of her little jokes.

But Yollie wasn't laughing. She tiptoed into her mother's bedroom with a glass of water and set it on the nightstand next to the alarm clock. The next morning, Yollie woke to screams. When her mother reached to turn off the alarm, she had overturned the glass of water.

Yollie burned her mother's morning toast and gloated. "Ha! Ha! I got you back. Why did you leave me on the couch when I told you to wake me up?"

Despite their jokes, mother and daughter usually got along. They watched bargain matinees together, and played croquet in the summer and checkers in the winter. Mrs. Moreno encouraged Yollie to study hard because she wanted her daughter to be a doctor. She bought Yollie a desk, a typewriter, and a lamp that cut glare so her eyes would not grow tired from hours of studying.

Yollie was slender as a tulip, pretty, and one of the smartest kids at Saint Theresa's. She was captain of crossing guards, an altar girl, and a whiz in the school's monthly spelling bees.

"Tienes que estudiar mucho," Mrs. Moreno said every time she propped her work-weary feet on the hassock. "You have to study a lot, then you can get a good job and take care of me."

"Yes, Mama," Yollie would respond, her face buried in a book. If she gave her mother any sympathy, she would begin her stories about how she had come with her family from Mexico with nothing on her back but a sack with three skirts, all of which were too large by the time she crossed the border because she had lost weight from not having enough to eat.

Everyone thought Yollie's mother was a riot. Even the nuns laughed at her antics. Her brother Raul, a nightclub owner, thought she was funny enough to go into show business.

But there was nothing funny about Yollie needing a new outfit for the eighth-grade fall dance. They couldn't afford one. It was late October, with Christmas around the corner, and their dented Chevy Nova had gobbled up almost one hundred dollars in repairs.

"We don't have the money," said her mother, genuinely sad because they couldn't buy the outfit, even though there was a little money stashed away for college. Mrs. Moreno remembered her teenage years and her hard-working parents, who picked grapes and oranges, and chopped beets and cotton for meager pay around Kerman. Those were the days when "new clothes" meant limp and out-of-style dresses from Saint Vincent de Paul.

The best Mrs. Moreno could do was buy Yollie a pair of black shoes with velvet bows and fabric dye to color her white summer dress black.

"We can color your dress so it will look brand-new," her mother said brightly, shaking the bottle of dye as she ran hot water into a plastic dish tub. She poured the black liquid into the tub and stirred it with a pencil. Then, slowly and carefully, she lowered the dress into the tub.

Yollie couldn't stand to watch. She *knew* it wouldn't work. It would be like the time her mother stirred up a batch of molasses for candy apples on Yollie's birthday. She'd dipped the apples into the goo and swirled them and seemed to taunt Yollie by singing ***"Las Mañanitas"*** to her. When she was through, she set the apples on wax paper. They were hard as rocks and hurt the kids' teeth. Finally they had a contest to see who could break the apples open by throwing them against the side of the house. The apples shattered like grenades, sending the kids scurrying for cover, and in an odd way the birthday party turned out to be a success. At least everyone went home happy.

To Yollie's surprise, the dress came out shiny black. It looked brand-new and sophisticated, like what people in New York wear. She beamed at her mother, who hugged Yollie and said, "See, what did I tell you?"

The dance was important to Yollie because she was in love with Ernie Castillo, the third-best speller in the class. She bathed, dressed, did her hair and nails, and primped until her mother yelled, "All right already." Yollie sprayed her neck and wrists with Mrs. Moreno's Avon perfume and bounced into the car.

Mrs. Moreno let Yollie out in front of the school. She waved and told her to have a good time but behave herself, then roared off, blue smoke trailing from the tailpipe of the old Nova.

 Stop here for the Strategy Break.

Strategy Break

What conclusions can you draw about Mrs. Moreno's character so far? If you were to begin a character map to list some of her traits, it might look like the one below. When you get to the end of the story, you will finish the map.

CHARACTER TRAIT:
strange sense of humor
Example:
She agrees to wake Yollie at the end of the movie, but she leaves her sleeping on the couch.

CHARACTER TRAIT:
fun-loving
Example:
She and Yollie watch bargain matinees and play croquet and checkers together. Her brother Raul thinks she is funny enough to go into show business.

Character: Mrs. Moreno

CHARACTER TRAIT:
resourceful
Example:
When her caramel apples are hard as rocks, she has a contest to see who can break them open. When she can't afford to buy Yollie a dress for the dance, she dyes Yollie's old one.

CHARACTER TRAIT:

As you continue reading, see what conclusions you draw about Yollie. You will create a character map for her in the Strategy Follow-up.

 Go on reading to see what happens.

Yollie ran into her best friend, Janice. They didn't say it, but each thought the other was the most beautiful girl at the dance; the boys would fall over themselves asking them to dance.

The evening was warm but thick with clouds. Gusts of wind picked up the paper lanterns hanging in the trees and swung them, blurring the night with reds and yellows. The lanterns made the evening seem romantic, like a scene from a movie. Everyone danced, sipped punch, and stood in knots of threes and fours, talking. Sister Kelly got up and jitterbugged with some kid's father. When the record ended, students broke into applause.

Janice had her eye on Frankie Ledesma, and Yollie, who kept smoothing her dress down when the wind picked up, had her eye on Ernie. It turned out that Ernie had his mind on Yollie, too. He ate a handful of cookies nervously, then asked her for a dance.

"Sure," she said, nearly throwing herself into his arms.

They danced two fast ones before they got a slow one. As they circled under the lanterns, rain began falling, lightly at first. Yollie loved the sound of the raindrops ticking against the leaves. She leaned her head on Ernie's shoulder, though his sweater was scratchy. He felt warm and tender. Yollie could tell that he was in love, and with her, of course. The dance continued successfully, romantically, until it began to pour.

"Everyone, let's go inside—and, boys, carry in the table and the record player," Sister Kelly commanded.

The girls and boys raced into the cafeteria. Inside, the girls, drenched to the bone, hurried to the restrooms to brush their hair and dry themselves. One girl cried because her velvet dress was ruined. Yollie felt sorry for her and helped her dry the dress off with paper towels, but it was no use. The dress was ruined.

Yollie went to a mirror. She looked a little gray now that her mother's makeup had washed away but not as bad as some of the other girls. She combed her damp hair, careful not to pull too hard. She couldn't wait to get back to Ernie.

Yollie bent over to pick up a bobby pin, and shame spread across her face. A black puddle was forming at her feet. Drip, black drip. Drip, black drip. The dye was falling from her dress like black tears. Yollie stood up. Her dress was now the color of ash. She looked around the room. The other girls, unaware of Yollie's problem, were busy grooming themselves. What could she do? Everyone would laugh. They would know she dyed an old dress because she couldn't afford a new one. She hurried from the restroom with her head down, across the cafeteria floor and out the door. She raced through the storm, crying as the rain mixed with her tears and ran into twig-choked gutters.

When she arrived home, her mother was on the couch eating cookies and watching TV.

"How was the dance, *m'ija*? Come watch the show with me. It's really good."

Yollie stomped, head down, to her bedroom. She undressed and threw the dress on the floor.

Her mother came into the room. "What's going on? What's all the racket, baby?"

"The dress. It's cheap! It's no good!" Yollie kicked the dress at her mother and watched it land in her hands. Mrs. Moreno studied it closely but couldn't see what was wrong. "What's the matter? It's just a bit wet."

"The dye came out, that's what."

Mrs. Moreno looked at her hands and saw the grayish dye puddling in the shallow lines of her palms. Poor baby, she thought, her brow darkening as she made a sad face. She wanted to tell her daughter how sorry she was, but she knew it wouldn't help. She walked back to the living room and cried.

The next morning, mother and daughter stayed away from each other. Yollie sat in her room turning the pages of an old *Seventeen*, while her mother watered her plants with a Pepsi bottle.

"Drink, my children," she said loud enough for Yollie to hear. She let the water slurp into pots of coleus and cacti. "Water is all you need. My daughter needs clothes, but I don't have no money."

Yollie tossed her *Seventeen* on her bed. She was embarrassed at last night's tirade. It wasn't her mother's fault that they were poor.

When they sat down together for lunch, they felt awkward about the night before. But Mrs. Moreno had made a fresh stack of tortillas and cooked up a pan of **chile verde**, and that broke the ice. She licked her thumb and smacked her lips.

"You know, honey, we gotta figure a way to make money," Yollie's mother said. "You and me. We don't have to be poor. Remember the Garcias. They made this stupid little tool that fixes cars. They moved away because they're rich. That's why we don't see them no more."

"What can we make?" asked Yollie. She took another tortilla and tore it in half.

"Maybe a screwdriver that works on both ends? Something like that." The mother looked around the room for ideas, but then shrugged. "Let's forget it. It's better to get an education. If you get a good job and have spare time then maybe you can invent something." She rolled her tongue over her lips and cleared her throat. "The county fair hires people. We can get a job there. It will be here next week."

Yollie hated the idea. What would Ernie say if he saw her pitching hay at the cows? How could she go to school smelling like an armful of chickens? "No, they wouldn't hire us," she said.

The phone rang. Yollie lurched from her chair to answer it, thinking it would be Janice wanting to know why she had left. But it was Ernie wondering the same thing. When he found out she wasn't mad at him, he asked if she would like to go to a movie.

"I'll ask," Yollie said, smiling. She covered the phone with her hand and counted to ten. She uncovered the receiver and said, "My mom says it's OK. What are we going to see?"

After Yollie hung up, her mother climbed, grunting, onto a chair to reach the top shelf in the hall closet. She wondered why she hadn't done it earlier. She reached behind a stack of towels and pushed her chubby hand into the cigar box where she kept her secret stash of money.

"I've been saving a little money every month," said Mrs. Moreno. "For you, *m'ija*." Her mother held up five twenties, a blossom of green that smelled sweeter than flowers on that Saturday. They drove to Macy's and bought a blouse, shoes, and a skirt that would not bleed in rain or any other kind of weather. ●

Strategy Follow-up

First go back and complete the character map for Mrs. Moreno. Then complete the following character map for Yollie.

CHARACTER TRAIT:	CHARACTER TRAIT:
Example:	Example:

Character: Yollie

CHARACTER TRAIT:	CHARACTER TRAIT:
Example:	Example:

✓ Personal Checklist

Read each question and put a check (✓) in the correct box.

1. How well do you understand what happens in "Mother and Daughter"?
   - ☐ 3 (extremely well)
   - ☐ 2 (fairly well)
   - ☐ 1 (not well)

2. After you read Building Background, how well were you able to understand why this story is told from the third-person point of view?
   - ☐ 3 (extremely well)
   - ☐ 2 (fairly well)
   - ☐ 1 (not well)

3. In the Vocabulary Builder, how well were you able to match the Spanish words with their definitions?
   - ☐ 3 (extremely well)
   - ☐ 2 (fairly well)
   - ☐ 1 (not well)

4. How well were you able to complete the character maps for Mrs. Moreno and Yollie?
   - ☐ 3 (extremely well)
   - ☐ 2 (fairly well)
   - ☐ 1 (not well)

5. How well do you understand the relationship between Mrs. Moreno and Yollie?
   - ☐ 3 (extremely well)
   - ☐ 2 (fairly well)
   - ☐ 1 (not well)

Vocabulary Check

Look back at the work you did in the Vocabulary Builder. Then answer each question by circling the correct letter.

1. Why do people call Mrs. Moreno *Mamacita*?
   a. They like her and wish she could be their mother.
   b. Since it means "little mother," they are making a joke.
   c. They think that Mrs. Moreno is their mother.

2. Why do you think Mrs. Moreno tells Yollie, *"Tienes que estudiar mucho"*?
   a. She wants Yollie to keep busy so she doesn't bother her.
   b. She wants Yollie to be able to get a good job.
   c. She thinks that Yollie is a very lazy girl.

3. Why does Mrs. Moreno sing *"Las Mañanitas"* while she makes the caramel apples?
   a. It's Yollie's birthday, so she sings her a birthday song.
   b. It's the only song for which she remembers all the words.
   c. It's a song about caramel apples, so it is appropriate.

4. Considering the title of this story, what do you think *m'ija* means in English?
   a. my dancer
   b. my student
   c. my daughter

5. What do Yollie and her mother do with *chile verde*?
   a. They eat it with tortillas.
   b. The use it to decorate Yollie's dress.
   c. They use it to cool the apartment.

Add the numbers that you just checked to get your Personal Checklist score. Fill in your score here. Then turn to page 209 and transfer your score onto Graph 1.

Personal
Vocabulary
Strategy
Comprehension
TOTAL SCORE
✓ T

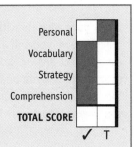

Check your answers with your teacher. Give yourself 1 point for each correct answer, and fill in your Vocabulary score here. Then turn to page 209 and transfer your score onto Graph 1.

Personal
Vocabulary
Strategy
Comprehension
TOTAL SCORE
✓ T

Strategy Check

Review the character maps for Mrs. Moreno and Yollie. Then answer these questions:

1. Which of the following character traits would you *not* include on a character map for Mrs. Moreno?

   a. angry

   b. strange sense of humor

   c. loving

2. Which example supports the conclusion that Mrs. Moreno is loving?

   a. She agrees to wake Yollie but leaves her sleeping on the couch.

   b. When Yollie has a date, she buys her a blouse, shoes, and a skirt.

   c. Her brother Raul thinks she is funny enough to go into show business.

3. Which of the following traits would *not* belong on a character map for Yollie?

   a. good student

   b. likes to joke

   c. spoiled brat

4. Which example supports the conclusion that Yollie is sensitive?

   a. She puts a glass of water on her mother's nightstand.

   b. After she yells at her mother, she feels embarrassed.

   c. She is a whiz in the monthly spelling bees.

5. What is one character trait that Mrs. Moreno and Yollie have in common?

   a. They are both fun-loving.

   b. They both study very hard.

   c. They are both resourceful.

Comprehension Check

Review the story if necessary. Then answer these questions:

1. Who is the third-person narrator in this story?

   a. Yollie

   b. Mrs. Moreno

   c. someone outside the story

2. Why did Yollie's birthday party turn out to be a success?

   a. The caramel apples were chewy and delicious.

   b. Everyone had fun breaking the apples against the house.

   c. Her mother had hired clowns and ponies.

3. How does Mrs. Moreno get Yollie a dress for the dance?

   a. She takes Yollie on a shopping spree.

   b. She borrows one from her niece.

   c. She dyes Yollie's summer dress.

4. Mrs. Moreno dyes a dress for Yollie that bleeds. How do you know this isn't one of Mrs. Moreno's strange jokes?

   a. She doesn't start laughing when Yollie gets home.

   b. Yollie doesn't play a joke back on Mrs. Moreno.

   c. Mrs. Moreno cries when she sees Yollie's dress.

5. Why do you think this story isn't called "Yollie's Dress"?

   a. because it really should be called "The Dance"

   b. because her relationship with her mother is more important

   c. because it really should be called "Yollie's New Clothes"

Check your answers with your teacher. Give yourself 1 point for each correct answer, and fill in your Strategy score here. Then turn to page 209 and transfer your score onto Graph 1.

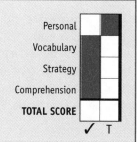

Check your answers with your teacher. Give yourself 1 point for each correct answer, and fill in your Comprehension score here. Then turn to page 209 and transfer your score onto Graph 1.

Extending

Choose one or more of these activities:

SKETCH A SCENE FROM THE STORY

Choose a favorite scene from this story and sketch it. Reread the scene and underline all of the descriptive details that help make it clearer for you. Include as many of those details in your sketch as possible.

ROLE-PLAY A SCENE

Imagine another interaction between Yollie and her mother. For example, imagine what will happen when Ernie brings Yollie home from their date. What will Yollie's mother do? Will she be polite and nice, or will she play some sort of embarrassing joke on Yollie? Consider what you know about Yollie and her mother as you plan what they will say and do. Discuss your ideas with a classmate or two, and then role-play the scene for the rest of the class.

READ OTHER WORKS BY GARY SOTO

Choose one of the books by Gary Soto that is listed on this page, and report on it to the class. You can make your report orally or in writing. If you'd like, read aloud or mention some of your favorite passages, and explain why they appeal to you.

Resources

Books

Soto, Gary, *Off and Running.* Bantam, 1997.

———. *Pacific Crossing.* Harcourt, 2003.

———. *The Pool Party.* Yearling Books, 1995.

———. *The Skirt.* Bt Bound, 1999.

Web Site

http://www.garysoto.com/index.html
This is the official Gary Soto Web site.

LESSON (4) Bears

Building Background

You have heard about bears and seen pictures of them ever since you were young. But how much do you really know about these animals? Are they as fierce as many people think? Do all bears look alike? Before you begin reading this selection, choose a partner and fill in the first column of the chart below with at least three things that you know about bears. Fill in the second column with at least three questions about bears that you hope the selection will answer. When you finish the selection, you will fill in the last column.

BEARS

K (What I Know)	W (What I Want to Know)	L (What I Learned)
1.	1.	1.
2.	2.	2.
3.	3.	3.

conservationists

habitats

hibernating

prey

Vocabulary Builder

1. The words in the margin are specialized vocabulary words. **Specialized vocabulary** words are all related to a particular topic in some way. For example, in this selection the words are all related to bears and the study of bears.

2. Sometimes using **context clues** helps you figure out a specialized vocabulary word. Read the sentences below, and underline the context clues that help you figure out the boldfaced words.
   a. When **hibernating**, a bear sleeps most of the time, but it may wake up and even leave the den for a few hours at a time.
   b. Most kinds of bears are quickly losing their **habitats**—the places where they can live in the wild.
   c. A polar bear can smell its favorite **prey**, or food, from miles away.
   d. Scientists and **conservationists** are working to find ways to help bears survive in the crowded modern world.

3. Save your work. You will refer to it again in the Vocabulary Check.

Strategy Builder

How to Read Nonfiction

- **Nonfiction** is writing that gives readers information about a particular subject, or topic. The **topic** is what a piece of writing is all about. The topic of the article that you are about to read is bears—kinds of bears, what they are like, and where they live.

- Like all other types of nonfiction, "Bears" follows a particular pattern of organization. (The most common patterns are listed in the margin.) In Lesson 2 the pattern of "The Parcel Post Kid" was sequence. The pattern that you'll find in "Bears" is description. A **description** usually explains what something is, what it does, or how and why it works.

- A description is usually organized according to **main ideas** and **supporting details**. For example, read the following paragraph. The topic, ants, is in bold print. Each new category, or main idea, that describes something about ants is underlined once. The details that support that main idea are underlined twice.

> **Ants** are insects that <u>live in communities called colonies</u>. Some colonies are in underground <u>tunnels</u>, while others are in <u>hills</u> above the ground or in <u>trees</u>. There <u>are three main kinds of ants</u>: <u>queens</u>, <u>workers</u>, and <u>males</u>. These ants have different jobs. <u>Queens lay eggs</u>. <u>Workers build and take care of the colony</u>, <u>search for food</u>, <u>and take care of the queen's eggs</u>. <u>Male ants mate with queen ants</u>. That is their only job. Soon after mating, male ants die.

- If you wanted to arrange this excerpt's main ideas and supporting details on a graphic organizer, you could use a **concept map**, or web. It would look something like this:

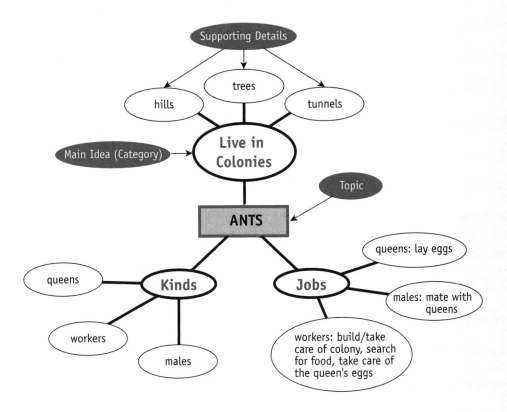

CLIPBOARD

Organization Patterns of Nonfiction

description

cause-effect

sequence

compare-contrast

Bears

by Dorothy Hinshaw Patent

As you begin reading "Bears," apply some of the strategies that you just learned. Look for the main ideas and supporting details in this description, and think about how you might organize them on a concept map.

Bears put smiles on our faces when we see them in zoos, and they live in our imaginations as characters from stories like *Goldilocks and the Three Bears* and *Winnie-the-Pooh*. But zoo bears and storybook bears don't tell us much about what bears are really like. Bears show their real selves only when living wild.

All bears are large and stocky with short, thick legs. They have short tails, small ears, pointed muzzles, and eyes that look straight ahead. Each bear foot has five toes. Bears walk the way we do, on the flat of the foot. When a bear stands up on its hind legs, it looks a lot like a furry person.

Bears are usually born in the winter den of the mother. They are tiny at birth; a newborn black bear cub, for example, weighs less than a pound. But the cubs grow fast on their mother's rich milk and are ready to explore when the time comes to leave the den. Young bears depend on their mother to teach them what they need to know to survive. They learn from her how to avoid danger and where to find food.

 Stop here for the Strategy Break.

Strategy Break

If you were to create a concept map for the information in this description so far, it might look like this:

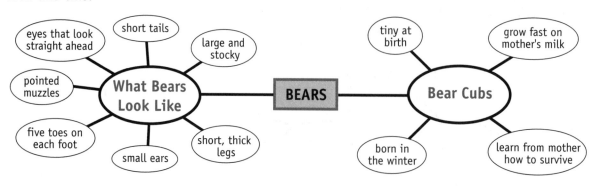

As you continue reading, keep paying attention to the main ideas and supporting details that describe bears. At the end of the selection you will use some of the information to complete a concept map of your own.

Go on reading.

Although we think of bears as meat eaters, most eat several different kinds of food. Grizzly bears, for instance, eat more grass and berries than meat. Bears can see and hear quite well. But their best sense is their sense of smell. A polar bear can smell a seal, its favorite **prey**, from miles away.

Most northern bears spend the long winters in dens. They enter a special condition called hibernation. When **hibernating**, a bear sleeps most of the time, but it may wake up and even leave the den for a few hours at a time.

There are just eight kinds of bears in the world. Four of these kinds live in Asia. The Malayan sun bear, with its wrinkled forehead and handsome yellow necklace, is popular in zoos. It is the smallest bear, just about the size of an adult person.

The shaggy sloth bear from India and Sri Lanka is twice the size of the sun bear. It feeds mostly on termites, using its long snout and flexible lips to suck up the insects after digging apart their nest with its sharp claws.

The charming black-and-white panda lives in the high mountains of China. Its front foot has an extra thumblike toe for holding on to the bamboo it eats. The Asiatic black bear is found in many parts of Asia and is similar to our American black bear.

The American black bear lives in woods throughout most of North America, from Alaska to Mexico and from Washington to Maine. Because it spends most of its life among trees, few people ever see a wild black bear. Black bears can actually be any number of colors, from almost white through many shades of brown to gleaming black.

The brown bear can also be almost any color from blond to black. Brown bears once lived all across the Northern Hemisphere and throughout most of what is now the western United States. But now these magnificent animals have disappeared from most states and are rare in western Europe. In North America, we call brown bears "grizzlies." The largest brown bears live on Kodiak Island in Alaska. A big Kodiak bear may stand 10 feet tall on its hind legs and weigh 1,700 pounds, as much as ten large people put together.

The giant polar bear is nearly as big as the Kodiak bear. Polar bears are designed for life in the cold northern polar regions. Their thick white fur soaks up the sunlight, and their huge paws act like snowshoes when they walk and like oars when they swim. A polar bear is a patient hunter.

It may sit for hours beside a seal's breathing hole in the ice, waiting for the seal to surface for air.

The spectacled bear is the only South American species. Its light-colored face has dark spots and often dark patches that look like eyeglasses, giving it its name. Spectacled bears are mountain dwellers that often climb trees to feed on fruit.

Most kinds of bears are quickly losing their **habitats**—the places where they can live in the wild—as humans take over more and more land. Asian bears, especially the giant panda, are the most threatened. Grizzly bears are found in only a few of the lower forty-eight states. But polar bears seem to be holding their own, American black bears are increasing in number, and grizzly bears are still plentiful in parts of Canada and Alaska. Scientists and **conservationists** are working with governments to find ways to help these intelligent and appealing animals survive in the crowded modern world. ●

Strategy Follow-up

First, work with your partner to fill in the last column of the chart on page 38. List at least three things that you learned about bears while reading this article.

Next, on a large sheet of paper, work with your partner to create a concept map for the eight kinds of bears in the world. Use the information for the Malayan sun bear as an example.

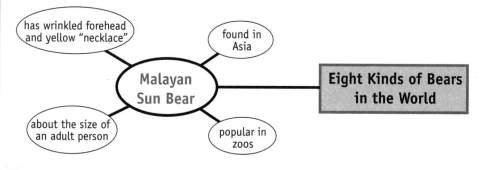

✓ Personal Checklist

Read each question and put a check (✓) in the correct box.

1. How well do you understand the information presented in this selection?
   - ☐ 3 (extremely well)
   - ☐ 2 (fairly well)
   - ☐ 1 (not well)

2. On the K-W-L chart, how easily were you and your partner able to list at least three things that you learned while reading this selection?
   - ☐ 3 (extremely easily)
   - ☐ 2 (fairly easily)
   - ☐ 1 (not easily)

3. In the Vocabulary Builder, how well were you able underline the context clues that helped you understand the specialized vocabulary words?
   - ☐ 3 (extremely well)
   - ☐ 2 (fairly well)
   - ☐ 1 (not well)

4. How well were you able to help your partner complete the concept map in the Strategy Follow-up?
   - ☐ 3 (extremely well)
   - ☐ 2 (fairly well)
   - ☐ 1 (not well)

5. After reading this selection, how well would you be able to describe bears and how they live?
   - ☐ 3 (extremely well)
   - ☐ 2 (fairly well)
   - ☐ 1 (not well)

Vocabulary Check

Look back at the work you did in the Vocabulary Builder. Then answer each question by circling the correct letter.

1. Which phrase best describes what a bear does while it is hibernating?
   a. spending the summer in sleep or inactivity
   b. spending the winter roaming the country
   c. spending the winter in sleep or inactivity

2. Which of the following is *not* a natural habitat of bears?
   a. zoo
   b. mountain
   c. ocean

3. What is one of the main reasons that bears are losing their habitats in the wild?
   a. They are being killed by other animals.
   b. People are taking more and more of their land.
   c. Forest fires are destroying their homes.

4. Which of the following is an action that a conservationist would *not* take?
   a. writing letters protesting unlimited bear hunting
   b. seeking laws to stop taking over bears' habitats
   c. killing bears in order to collect and sell their skins

5. Which word describes animals that bears hunt for food?
   a. prey
   b. dens
   c. cubs

Add the numbers that you just checked to get your Personal Checklist score. Fill in your score here. Then turn to page 209 and transfer your score onto Graph 1.

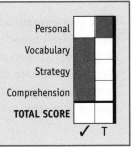

Check your answers with your teacher. Give yourself 1 point for each correct answer, and fill in your Vocabulary score here. Then turn to page 209 and transfer your score onto Graph 1.

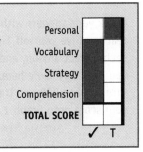

Strategy Check

Review the concept map that you and your partner created for the eight kinds of bears. Then answer these questions:

1. Which of these bears does *not* live in Asia?
   a. giant polar bear
   b. Malayan sun bear
   c. panda bear

2. Which bear is the only South American species?
   a. spectacled bear
   b. sloth bear
   c. brown bear

3. For which bear did you list the detail "patient hunter"?
   a. American black bear
   b. giant polar bear
   c. Malayan sun bear

4. In North America, what is another name for a brown bear?
   a. panda bear
   b. grizzly bear
   c. sloth bear

5. Which of these details could you have listed for the American black bear?
   a. seen by very few people
   b. has patches that look like eyeglasses
   c. feeds mostly on termites

Comprehension Check

Review the selection if necessary. Then answer these questions:

1. Where are bears usually born?
   a. in zoos around the world
   b. in the forests of Asia
   c. in their mother's winter den

2. Which of a bear's senses is the keenest, or sharpest?
   a. sight
   b. hearing
   c. smell

3. In the sentence, "Bears cubs are ready to explore when the time comes to leave the den," what does the word *den* mean?
   a. family room
   b. cave
   c. headquarters

4. Which bears are in the most danger of losing their habitats?
   a. American black bears
   b. polar bears
   c. giant pandas

5. Which sentence best describes why the work of conservationists, scientists, and government agencies is important?
   a. There are just eight kinds of bears in the world.
   b. Bears put smiles on our faces when we see them in zoos.
   c. Most kinds of bears are quickly losing their habitats.

Check your answers with your teacher. Give yourself 1 point for each correct answer, and fill in your Strategy score here. Then turn to page 209 and transfer your score onto Graph 1.

Personal	
Vocabulary	
Strategy	
Comprehension	
TOTAL SCORE	
	✓ T

Check your answers with your teacher. Give yourself 1 point for each correct answer, and fill in your Comprehension score here. Then turn to page 209 and transfer your score onto Graph 1.

Personal	
Vocabulary	
Strategy	
Comprehension	
TOTAL SCORE	
	✓ T

Extending

Choose one or more of these activities:

MAP OUT THE BEARS' LOCATIONS

Draw an outline map of the world, or trace one from a reference book. Then, using the information on your concept map, find the general locations of the eight kinds of bears. Using eight different colored pencils or markers, label each location and write the name of the bear or bears that live there.

CREATE AN INFORMATIONAL PICTURE BOOK

Some of the fun of learning new information is being able to share it with others. Create an informational picture book about bears that you can share with your classmates or younger children. Use the information in "Bears," as well as some of the sources listed on this page. If you'd like, draw a concept map to help you organize the information that you plan to include in your book.

FIND OUT ABOUT SAVING WILD ANIMALS

Find out more about conservationists and how they are trying to protect wild animals. Log on to the Internet, or go to the library to get more information. Then design a poster or pamphlet that tells about conservationists and their work.

Resources

Books

Crewe, Subrina, and Robert Morton. *The Bear.* Life Cycles. Raintree/Steck-Vaughn, 1997.

Hobbs, Will. *Beardance.* HarperTrophy, 1999.

———. *Bearstone.* HarperTrophy, 1997.

Lynch, Wayne (photographer). *Bears, Bears, Bears.* Firefly Books, 1995.

Stirling, Ian, and Aubrey Lang (photographer). *Bears.* Sierra Club for Children. 1992.

Web Sites

http://www.bears.org/
Learn facts about various species of bears on this Web site.

http://www.nwf.org/wildlifework/
This Web site discusses efforts to conserve wildlife.

http://www.polarbearsalive.org/facts2.php
This Web site provides information on polar bears.

A Greenland Rope Trick

Building Background

Have you ever imagined that you were stranded alone in the wilderness with little more than your courage and wits to help you survive? Have you wondered what you would do? The story you are about to read is based on actual events. It tells about a boy who gets stranded on a piece of Arctic ice that breaks off from the land and floats out to the sea. What do you predict he might do to try and survive?

aurora borealis

floe

hummocks

nimbus

nubble

squall

Vocabulary Builder

1. The vocabulary words in Column 1 are all related to the **setting** of "The Greenland Rope Trick." Before you begin reading the story, use a dictionary to find the definitions of the words. Then draw a line from each word in Column 1 to its definition in Column 2.

COLUMN 1	COLUMN 2
aurora borealis	lump or small piece
floe	bright cloud around something
hummocks	small, round hills
nimbus	colorful bands of light across the northern sky
nubble	sudden, violent storm or gust of wind
squall	sheet of floating ice

2. Save your work. You will refer to it again in the Vocabulary Check.

Strategy Builder

Mapping the Elements of a Story

- One of the main elements of every story is its plot. The **plot** is the sequence of events in a story. In most stories, the plot revolves around a problem that the main character or characters have and the steps they take to solve it.

- Another element is the **setting**—the time and place in which the story happens. In some stories the setting is a major element, as it is in "A Greenland Rope Trick." The setting greatly influences what happens in this story.

- A good way to keep track of what happens in a story is to record its elements on a **story map**. Study the story map below. It lists and defines the elements that you should be looking for as you read a story.

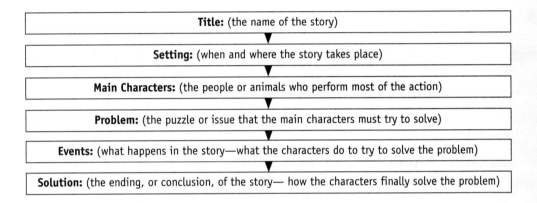

Title: (the name of the story)

▼

Setting: (when and where the story takes place)

▼

Main Characters: (the people or animals who perform most of the action)

▼

Problem: (the puzzle or issue that the main characters must try to solve)

▼

Events: (what happens in the story—what the characters do to try to solve the problem)

▼

Solution: (the ending, or conclusion, of the story— how the characters finally solve the problem)

A Greenland Rope Trick

by K.C. Tessendorf
based on a true story

As you begin reading this story, apply the strategies that you just learned. Keep track of the characters, setting, and other elements. You may want to underline them as you read.

Ordinarily, Metok would have been too young to accompany the men of Upernivik on the walrus hunt. But his father had been laid up by the swat of a polar bear's paw, and now the boy was slogging with the other hunters fifteen miles over sea ice to open water in Baffin Bay.

The February sea lay black under the sunless winter sky. Starlight, a pale southern moon, and the flickering shafts of the **aurora borealis** showed the walrus herd out in the water, not resting on the ice where the hunters could harpoon them.

The hunters decided to try luring in a bull walrus and hid behind low ice **hummocks** near the edge of the open water. One of the men bellowed out a sonorous *U-R-L-K! U-R-L-K!* With luck, the dominant male would leave his females and return to the ice to deal with a rival bull. Today, though, there was no response, and soon the senior hunter pointed at the white **nimbus** waxing about the moon. "The wind comes," he said. "We must go back."

Metok lagged behind as the men headed toward land with their dogs and sledges. When they were far enough ahead, the boy turned back and hid behind a hummock by the water. He hoped that the walruses, seeing their enemies leaving, would come onto the ice where he could surprise and kill one. How the elders would praise him! He waited patiently, but the walrus herd only continued swimming in the calm sea.

All of a sudden the boy became aware of a violent **squall** of wind-driven snow hissing outward from the land. Alarmed, he ran to his dogs and sled and pointed the team into the gale sweeping down from the Greenland ice cap. A rending *crack!* filled the air, and Metok saw the ice pack split ahead. Desperately, the boy sprinted ahead of his dogs.

Too late! The widening water was too broad for Metok to leap across. But the dogs, heeding instinct, rushed past and plunged into the icy water. They managed to swim across the break and drag the sled out behind them. Then they ran off into the steam and snow haze, leaving Metok stranded.

The ice **floe** bearing its prisoner began to heave gently as it drifted out to sea. Metok knew if he abandoned hope now, he would freeze to death within hours. But his people, the Inuit, had not lived thousands of years in the Arctic without learning to survive in their harsh environment.

Beating his arms and jumping to maintain blood flow, the boy took stock. For tools, he had only his long sheath knife and the fire flint he carried inside his parka. He looked around and glimpsed a tall knob of ice, a fragment of glacier, near the center of the floe. Using his knife, the boy quickly cut snow blocks to build an igloo shelter on one side of the knob. He drew a block to plug the hole behind him and, dressed in his warm sealskin parka, slept until the outside storm subsided.

 Stop here for the Strategy Break.

Strategy Break

Title: The Greenland Rope Trick

Setting: February in Baffin Bay, in the frozen Arctic, west of Greenland

Main Character(s): Metok

Problem: Metok is stranded on a drifting ice floe and needs to survive.

Events:
1. Metok and some others are out hunting walrus.
2. When the wind comes, the hunters decide to go back home.
3. Metok hides behind a hummock in hopes of catching a walrus.
4. A violent storm cracks the ice where Metok is standing.
5. He starts drifting out to sea on an ice floe.
6. He quickly builds an igloo and falls asleep until the storm passes.

To be continued...

As you continue reading, keep paying attention to the events in this story. You will complete the story map in the Strategy Follow-up.

 Go on reading to see what happens.

Metok floated south and west on his few acres of ice. Beneath the stars, moon, and flickering aurora, he saw only the black open sea of Baffin Bay. Finally, a dark shape appeared on the edge of the ice, and a ring seal climbed out of the water to rest. By now Metok was ravenously hungry, and he knew that he'd have to get within arm's length if he was to kill the creature.

The boy's father had long ago taught him how to stalk a seal by becoming one. Flopping down on his stomach, Metok began to wriggle in an awkward, zigzag fashion, like a seal on land. He bobbed his head and raised one elbow like a flipper. The sleepy seal, napping in snatches of ten to twenty seconds, gazed about dully between dozes. It thought Metok was another one of its kind out on the ice.

Face averted, Metok slithered closer. Then, grasping his knife, he abruptly rolled over and stabbed the animal. He didn't let go until he was sure the seal was dead.

Famished, Metok feasted on the raw meat before skinning and cutting up the rest of the seal for later. From its bones he crafted a disk lamp. He twisted strands of fur from his parka collar for a wick. Seal blubber provided fuel. Metok struck a spark from his fire flint, and a light blossomed within his igloo.

Later the boy killed a large bearded seal that had crawled onto the floe. Whatever peril lay ahead now, he was well stocked with seal meat. He cut thin strips of rawhide and wove and tied them to make a thick, strong, harpoon-length rope. Although he still needed a lance shaft, he was as prepared as possible.

The moon returned to hover above the southern horizon. In its white light, Metok saw a smaller ice floe drifting southeast toward his own. The boy grew cold with fear, for another lonely traveler was pacing about over there—Nanuk! The enormous polar bear was very thin, surely famished. The boy knew the bear had scented him when it reared up, standing eight feet or more, and began to weave its sleek head, sniffing avidly. Soon the bear would plunge into the icy water and come after him. With only his sheath knife, Metok could not expect to survive.

Metok recalled polar bears' strong preference for seal flesh. His father was still alive because of it. He'd been busy with a seal when Nanuk came from behind and disabled him with one mighty forearm swipe. Thereafter the bear ignored him, for it was the seal meat it wanted.

Metok had a store of meat left, and now he ran to dump an armload at the edge of the ice. Nanuk crouched across the narrowing channel, growling and slapping at the water. Seeing the seal meat, the polar bear plunged into the sea and swam to its dinner. Climbing onto Metok's floe, the bear roared with hunger and began to gorge itself.

When the meat was gone, Nanuk eyed Metok fearlessly yet without hostility. A heavy stomach had dulled the great bear's curiosity, and soon it lay down to sleep off the feast. Now Metok had time to think of what he would do when the bear awoke.

The boy considered an attack. He thought he could creep up on the bear, but then he'd have to climb onto it to stab at close quarters. Metok would be slashed by the aroused giant's claws and crushed by its great weight.

But what about his length of rawhide rope? The boy formed a plan as Nanuk slept on.

With his knife, Metok chipped a groove around a solid ice **nubble** near the igloo. He tied one end of the rope firmly around the notch, then spread the slack line out on top of the ice. Finally he tied a slip noose, burying the snare shallowly in the snow.

Hours later Nanuk awakened, stood up, and looked around for its servant. The boy obediently trotted out with a big load of meat, dumping it close to the hidden noose. Growling, Nanuk shuffled to the food and again gorged itself. Then it turned its attention to the boy, who stood backed up at the verge of the black, frigid sea, gripping his knife resolutely.

Black nose twitching, the bear stood for a long moment, evaluating this strange servant who provided raw seal meat. Finally the beast turned back to pick half-heartedly at the remnants of the feast before lying down again and closing its eyes.

Metok waited until he was sure the bear was sleeping. Then he began the hunting stalk of his young life, smoothly creeping upwind until at last he crouched, heart thumping, within a yard of slumbering Nanuk. Carefully he retrieved his noose. The bear's muzzle was flat on the ice, but a clever slap of the rope on its face, and the bear raised its head. Metok flipped the noose over Nanuk's head, gave a strong, quick jerk, and dashed toward the ice nubble.

Roaring, Nanuk galloped after Metok. The bear chased the boy in toward the nubble and back out again along the rope's length. Suddenly the snub of the tether crashed the giant to the ice, where it lay thrashing desperately, the rawhide rope pinching its windpipe shut. The great bear tumbled about, batting with its mighty paws until strangulation slowed its movements. Then the cunning hunter finished Nanuk with his knife.

For some time, the boy lived comfortably on his ice island, resting on a bearskin couch in a fur-lined igloo lit by two blubber lamps, From the bear's bones, he crafted a harpoon lance, which greatly eased his hunting chores.

Then the wind began blowing persistently from the south, raising the castaway's hopes. He was elated when his floe crunched against the Greenland shore ice and he was able to escape.

It took Metok a couple of weeks to hike back to his home village, dragging his ample meat in a bearskin behind him. By this time Metok's family and friends thought he was dead and, according to Inuit custom, had struck his name from conversation and group memory—but they were very happy to change their minds and welcome him home. ●

Strategy Follow-up

Now complete the story map for "A Greenland Rope Trick." (Use a separate sheet of paper if you need to.) Start with Event 7. Parts of the events have been filled in for you.

Problem: Metok is stranded on a drifting ice floe and needs to survive.

▼

Event 7: Metok kills a seal and

▼

Event 8: When Nanuk the polar bear approaches,

▼

Event 9: While Nanuk sleeps the first time,

▼

Event 10: While Nanuk sleeps the second time,

▼

Event 11: When Nanuk awakens

▼

Event 12: When Metok's ice floe crunches against the Greenland shore,

▼

Solution: After a couple of weeks

✓Personal Checklist

Read each question and put a check (✓) in the correct box.

1. How well do you understand what the title of this story means?
   - ☐ 3 (extremely well)
   - ☐ 2 (fairly well)
   - ☐ 1 (not well)

2. In Building Background, how well were you able to predict what Metok might do to survive?
   - ☐ 3 (extremely well)
   - ☐ 2 (fairly well)
   - ☐ 1 (not well)

3. In the Vocabulary Builder, how well were you able to match the vocabulary words and their definitions?
   - ☐ 3 (extremely well)
   - ☐ 2 (fairly well)
   - ☐ 1 (not well)

4. How well were you able to complete the story map in the Strategy Follow-up?
   - ☐ 3 (extremely well)
   - ☐ 2 (fairly well)
   - ☐ 1 (not well)

5. Now that you've read this story, how well do you understand some of the ways of the Inuit?
   - ☐ 3 (extremely well)
   - ☐ 2 (fairly well)
   - ☐ 1 (not well)

Vocabulary Check

Look back at the work you did in the Vocabulary Builder. Then answer each question by circling the correct letter.

1. Which phrase does *not* relate to a squall?
   a. a calm sky
   b. a sudden storm
   c. strong winds

2. Which phrase relates to aurora borealis?
   a. beautiful sunset in the western sky
   b. bright, glowing ring around the moon
   c. colorful lights in the northern sky

3. Which phrase defines the word *floe*?
   a. floating ice
   b. grassy meadow
   c. rolling hills

4. Which phrase describes a hummock?
   a. hanging bed between two trees
   b. ridge of small, round hills
   c. large body of icy water

5. Which phrase defines *nimbus*?
   a. bright cloud around something
   b. large mass of floating ice
   c. sudden and violent storm

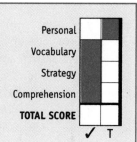

Add the numbers that you just checked to get your Personal Checklist score. Fill in your score here. Then turn to page 209 and transfer your score onto Graph 1.

Personal / Vocabulary / Strategy / Comprehension / TOTAL SCORE

Check your answers with your teacher. Give yourself 1 point for each correct answer, and fill in your Vocabulary score here. Then turn to page 209 and transfer your score onto Graph 1.

Personal / Vocabulary / Strategy / Comprehension / TOTAL SCORE

Strategy Check

Review the story map that you completed in the Strategy Follow-up. Then answer these questions:

1. What does Metok do when Nanuk approaches his ice floe?
   a. He slips a noose around its neck.
   b. He gives it some seal meat.
   c. He kills it with his knife.

2. When does Metok set a trap for Nanuk?
   a. while Nanuk sleeps the first time
   b. while Nanuk sleeps the second time
   c. while Nanuk eats the first time

3. What does Metok do while Nanuk sleeps the second time?
   a. He eats some of his seal meat.
   b. He sets a trap with his rope.
   c. He slips a noose around Nanuk's neck.

4. When is Metok able to escape his ice floe?
   a. when Nanuk chases him off of it
   b. when it crunches against the Greenland shore
   c. when his family sees him and welcomes him

5. What is the final solution to Metok's problem?
   a. He kills a seal and feasts on it.
   b. He slips a noose around Nanuk's neck.
   c. He makes it back home again.

Comprehension Check

Review the story if necessary. Then answer these questions:

1. Why do you think the author called this story "A Greenland Rope Trick"?
   a. It's a clue that Metok will trick Nanuk with a rope.
   b. It's a clue that Metok will learn some rope tricks.
   c. It's a clue that Metok will use a rope from Greenland.

2. Why is Metok on the seal hunt at such a young age?
   a. He is a very clever hunter.
   b. He is going without permission.
   c. He is taking his father's place.

3. How does Metok end up on the ice floe?
   a. The floe breaks off during a squall.
   b. He gets to it in his canoe.
   c. His dogs drag him there.

4. Why are seals so important to Metok?
   a. He uses them for food, fuel, and rope.
   b. They keep him company on the floe.
   c. They lead the floe back to land.

5. How does Metok keep Nanuk from killing him?
   a. He keeps it happy by feeding it.
   b. He tricks it and then kills it.
   c. Both of the above answers are correct.

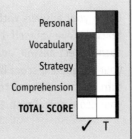

Check your answers with your teacher. Give yourself 1 point for each correct answer, and fill in your Strategy score here. Then turn to page 209 and transfer your score onto Graph 1.

Personal
Vocabulary
Strategy
Comprehension
TOTAL SCORE
✓ T

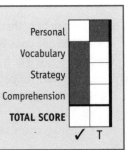

Check your answers with your teacher. Give yourself 1 point for each correct answer, and fill in your Comprehension score here. Then turn to page 209 and transfer your score onto Graph 1.

Personal
Vocabulary
Strategy
Comprehension
TOTAL SCORE
✓ T

LESSON 5: A GREENLAND ROPE TRICK

Extending

Choose one or more of these activities:

WRITE A SEQUEL TO THIS STORY

Continue Metok's adventures by writing about what happens after he returns home. Use a story map to plan your story. When you have finished writing it, dramatize it or read it aloud with a few of your classmates.

ILLUSTRATE THIS STORY

With a partner, create illustrations for this story. To make your pictures as realistic as possible, you might research Baffin Bay to find out what the area looks like. You also might find information on the Inuit, such as what they wear, what their homes are like, and what their hunting tools look like. Some of the resources on this page might help you get started.

READ ANOTHER SURVIVAL STORY

Read or listen to one of the books listed on this page or one you find yourself. Then give an oral or written report on the book. If another classmate chooses the same book, you might want to report on it together.

Resources

Books

George, Jean Craighead. *Julie of the Wolves.* HarperTrophy, 1974.

———. *On the Far Side of the Mountain.* Puffin, 2001.

Meyer, Carolyn. *In a Different Light: Growing Up in a Yup'ik Eskimo Village in Alaska.* Margaret K. McElderry, 1996.

Osinski, Alice. *The Eskimo: The Inuit and Yupik People.* New True Books. Children's Book Press, 1985.

Paulsen, Gary. *Brian's Return.* Laurel Leaf, 2001.

———. *Brian's Winter.* Laurel Leaf, 1998.

———. *Hatchet.* Simon Pulse, 1999.

Audio Recordings

Paulsen, Gary. *Brian's Return.* Bantam Books-Audio, 1999.

———. *Brian's Winter.* Bantam Books-Audio, 1996.

———. *Hatchet.* Bantam Books-Audio, 1992.

Learning New Words

VOCABULARY

From Lesson 1
- corral
- loft

From Lesson 5
- squall

Multiple-Meaning Words

A single word can have more than one meaning. For example, the word *squall* can mean "violent storm or gust of wind," "disturbance or commotion," or "loud, harsh cry." To figure out which meaning of *squall* an author is using, you have to use context. Context is the information surrounding a word or situation that helps you understand it.

When you read "A Greenland Rope Trick" you used context clues—including the setting of the story—to figure out that the meaning of *squall* was "violent storm or gust of wind."

Now use context to figure out the correct meaning of each underlined word. Circle the letter of the correct meaning.

1. Michelle's art gallery is located in the <u>loft</u> of a beautiful old building in the city.
   a. upper floor of a building or warehouse
   b. room under the roof of a barn

2. We put the horses in the <u>corral</u> after we gave them a good run.
   a. circle of wagons used to defend against attack
   b. pen built to keep animals in

3. Mr. Jacobs dug a deep hole for the fence <u>post</u>.
   a. place where a soldier is stationed
   b. piece of lumber or metal used as a support

4. Both sides of the debate team argued their <u>points</u> very well.
   a. main ideas
   b. tiny dots

5. My little sister stared at the fish swimming in the crystal clear <u>spring</u>.
   a. season of the year
   b. small stream of water

Compound Words

From Lesson 2
- postmaster

A compound word is made up of two words put together. For example, the word *postmaster* is made of the words *post* and *master*. When you read "The Parcel Post Kid," you learned that a *postmaster* is the person in charge of a post office.

Fill in each blank with a compound word by combining a word from Row 1 with a word from Row 2.

Row 1:	swim	ash	flash	under	tear
Row 2:	light	shirt	drop	tray	suit

1. tool used to see in the dark = _____

2. clothing worn beneath a top or jacket = _____

3. small dish used by smokers = _____

4. liquid that flows from the eye = _____

5. clothing worn at the beach = _____

Suffixes

A suffix is a word part that is added to the end of a root word. When you add a suffix, you often change the root word's meaning and function. For example, the suffix *-ful* means "full of," so the root word *joy* changes from a noun to an adjective meaning "full of joy."

-ist

The suffix *-ist* turns a word into a noun that means "a person who _____" or "a person who studies _____." In the selection "Bears," you learned that a *conservationist* is a person who works to conserve, or protect, the environment.

Draw a line from each word to its definition.

environmentalist	an expert in science
tourist	person who helps the environment
organist	an expert in chemistry
chemist	person who goes on a tour
scientist	person who plays the organ

VOCABULARY

From Lesson 4
- conservationists

LESSON 6 The Mysterious Treasure of Oak Island

Building Background

"The Mysterious Treasure of Oak Island" is **nonfiction**. As you learned in Lesson 2 nonfiction is based on facts, true events, and real people. Recognizing the **author's purpose** for writing a selection will help you understand it better. Authors write for one or more of these purposes: to **inform** (explain or describe something), to **persuade** (try to get you to agree with their opinion), to **entertain** (make you laugh or smile), and to **express** (share their feelings or ideas about something).

Based on the title of this selection, for what purpose or purposes do you predict Seymour Simon wrote "The Mysterious Treasure of Oak Island"?

expeditions

furiously

incredible

planks

platform

pulley

shaft

Vocabulary Builder

1. The words in the margin are from "The Mysterious Treasure of Oak Island." Before you begin reading this selection, think about what each word means. Then, on a separate sheet of paper, try to use each word in a sentence about hunting for buried treasure. If you're unsure of a word, guess for now. You'll have a chance to revise your sentences later.

2. As you read the selection, find the boldfaced vocabulary words. Use context clues to figure out what each word means, or look it up in a dictionary. If a word has more than one meaning, be sure to choose the one that fits the selection. Then return to your sentences and revise them if necessary.

3. Save your work. You will refer to it again in the Vocabulary Check.

Strategy Builder

Following Sequence While You Read

- "The Mysterious Treasure of Oak Island" follows the organizational pattern of **sequence**. It describes a series of events in the order in which they happened.

- To make the sequence of events as clear as possible, the author has used **signal words**. Some examples of signal words are *first, next, after that, in 1912,* and *the following year.*

- See if you can follow the sequence of events in the following paragraphs. Use the underlined signal words to help you.

> "There's a strong storm moving in from the west," said the radio announcer. "Better head undercover before it hits your area."
>
> <u>Upon hearing the radio report</u>, the lifeguards blew their whistles and got everyone out of the pool. <u>Then</u> they moved everyone into the changing rooms. <u>Next</u>, they closed the umbrellas and tipped the chairs so the wind would not blow them away.
>
> <u>After the storm passed</u>, the guards blew three long whistles, and everyone jumped back into the pool. The splash they made was almost as loud as the thunder.

- If you wanted to track the sequence of events in these paragraphs, you could put them on a **sequence chain**. It might look like this:

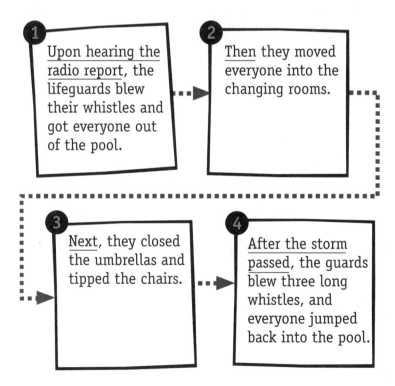

The Mysterious Treasure of Oak Island

by Seymour Simon

As you begin reading this selection, apply the strategies that you just learned. Pay attention to the signal words. They will give you a more exact picture of the sequence of events.

Buried treasure is usually difficult to find. Either there are no maps that show the location or the maps are poorly drawn and inaccurate. The only mystery surrounding most hidden treasures is summed up by the word *where*.

But there is one treasure in the world that doesn't fit these rules. You can get an exact map that shows the treasure spot. You can get photographs and measurements of the burial place. And you can even get there easily by plane and boat.

The treasure is located on Oak Island, a small spot in Mahone Bay off the southern shore of Nova Scotia in Canada. The island has even become a tourist attraction, with many people visiting the site of the treasure each year.

Yet for nearly two hundred years the buried treasure has remained on the island. Many digging **expeditions** and millions of dollars have been spent in trying to get to the treasure. But so far almost nothing has been recovered. The treasure of Oak Island remains a mystery that has not been solved.

The beginnings of the mystery date back to October, 1795. A teen-age boy, Dan McGinnis, had paddled a canoe over to Oak Island. At that time, nobody lived on the island.

McGinnis began to walk around the island through some of its oak forests. He came to a clearing and sat down to rest. Then he noticed something very odd. Beneath a large oak in the middle of the clearing, the soil had settled down into a pit several feet deep. And right above the pit, a large branch showed the remains of a **pulley**.

McGinnis became very excited. Could this be a spot where treasure had been buried? The next day McGinnis returned to the island with two of his friends, Anthony Vaughan and Jack Smith. They carried picks and shovels with them.

They were convinced that a treasure lay beneath the surface of the ground in the pit that McGinnis had discovered. They began to dig

furiously. Hour after hour they dug down into the pit. The deeper they dug, the more and more excited they became. They could see that they were digging down a **shaft** in the hard clay soil.

It was early evening when they made the next exciting discovery. By that time they had dug down ten feet. Just below their feet they saw a **platform** of heavy wooden **planks** laid side by side. The treasure must surely be right beneath, they thought.

It was too dark to keep digging, so they decided to return the next day. Early the next morning, the boys were back at the pit. They removed the planks from the pit one by one. But instead of a treasure beneath the planks, they found only more soil.

Again they began to dig, day after day. Finally they were down another ten feet, twenty feet below the surface. There they found another platform of wooden planks. But when they removed the layer of planks they found only more soil.

They continued to dig until the winter weather prevented them from going any further. By this time the hole was thirty feet deep. They had found still another platform of wooden planks at the thirty-foot level.

By now the boys were convinced that there must be a great treasure buried in the pit. Why else would anyone dig so far down and set up the wooden platforms?

The next spring the three began to dig again. The work was much more difficult now. The pit was very deep and all the soil had to be removed by buckets, pulleys, and ropes. Still they found no treasure, only another platform of wooden planks every ten feet down.

 Stop here for the Strategy Break.

Strategy Break

If you were to create a sequence chain to show the most important events in this selection so far, it might look like the one below. Notice the underlined signal words.

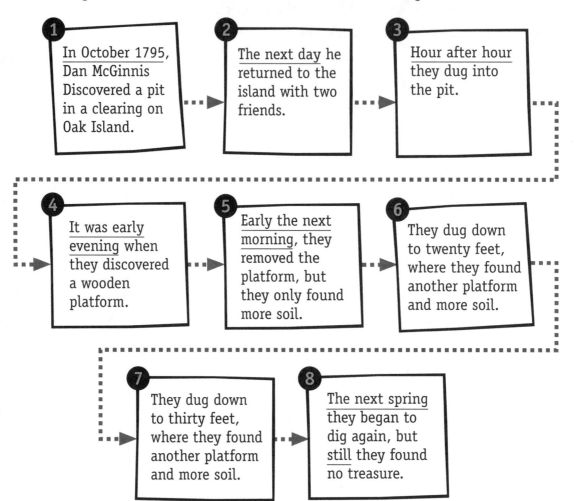

1 <u>In October 1795,</u> Dan McGinnis Discovered a pit in a clearing on Oak Island.

2 <u>The next day</u> he returned to the island with two friends.

3 <u>Hour after hour</u> they dug into the pit.

4 <u>It was early evening</u> when they discovered a wooden platform.

5 <u>Early the next morning,</u> they removed the platform, but they only found more soil.

6 They dug down to twenty feet, where they found another platform and more soil.

7 They dug down to thirty feet, where they found another platform and more soil.

8 <u>The next spring</u> they began to dig again, but <u>still</u> they found no treasure.

As you continue reading, keep paying attention to the sequence of events. Also keep looking for signal words. At the end of this selection, you will use some of them to complete a sequence chain of your own.

 Go on reading.

The digging went on for years. The boys grew up and had to take jobs to support themselves. But they dug in the pit whenever they could. Both McGinnis and Smith got married and took their brides to Oak Island to live in small houses they had built.

In 1804, nine years after the first discovery, a company was formed to dig down in the pit. The three boys, now men, worked for the company, which used all kinds of mining equipment as well as the help of other workers.

Deeper and deeper they went. Every ten feet down, they found another wooden platform laid exactly across the pit. Deeper in the shaft they found a layer of ship-waterproofing putty, then a layer of charcoal, and a third layer of a fiber that grows only in the tropics. But still they found no treasure.

The shaft was ninety-five feet deep when something new happened. The workers had finished for the day and had left. When they came back the next morning they found that sixty feet of water had flooded the pit.

But the workers did not give up. They used buckets to try to bail out the water. Day after day they bailed. But the water level remained the same. For every bucket the workers bailed out, another bucket of water had flooded in from somewhere.

Still the workers did not give up. They decided to dig another shaft nearby. Perhaps that way they could get to the level of the treasure. The new shaft went down one hundred and ten feet. But when the workers dug sideways to look for the treasure, water flooded into the new shaft and filled it to the same level as the old shaft.

That was the last straw. The company could do no more. All they had to show after months of difficult digging was two water-filled holes.

Years passed. The three original discoverers grew old. Yet they still believed in the treasure. The story of the Oak Island treasure had spread by that time. Other people began to believe that something must be buried in the "money pit."

The next big effort began in August of 1849. A group of businessmen and engineers decided to use the most modern equipment of the time to dig down in the pit.

They began to use a drill which picked up samples of whatever it passed through. At about one hundred feet, the drill went through another layer of wooden planks. Then it hit something else. It seemed to be loose metal. Was this the treasure? It is said that when the drill was brought to the surface it contained bits of a golden chain.

But the problem of getting rid of the water remained. Finally, after months of trying to solve the water problem, the group ran out of money and quit. The treasure was still beneath the ground.

Since that time, group after group has dug in the mine. Tunnel after tunnel has been built to drain away the water. Dynamite, bulldozers, electric pumps, and all kinds of equipment have been pressed into service. But all have failed. The water remains and the hidden treasure has not been found.

In 1965, a tragedy struck the digging. Four people were overcome by the fumes from a motor pump and died.

Still the explorations went on. A completely new shaft was dug two hundred feet away from the money pit. This new shaft reached what seemed to be a large hole far beneath the island.

A television camera was lowered into the water-filled hole. One of the watchers claims that he saw a chest in the dark waters. He claims that he also saw part of a human hand.

To this day, no one knows for sure if there is any treasure one hundred feet down in the money pit. Yet someone had to build the shaft and put the wooden platforms in place. Why would anyone go to all that trouble unless some **incredible** treasure was buried there? ●

Strategy Follow-up

Work with a partner or a small group to complete this activity. On a large sheet of paper, create a sequence chain for the second part of this selection. Begin with event 9. Underline any signal words that you include.

✓Personal Checklist

Read each question and put a check (✓) in the correct box.

1. How well do you understand the information in this selection?
   - ☐ 3 (extremely well)
   - ☐ 2 (fairly well)
   - ☐ 1 (not well)

2. In Building Background, how well were you able to predict the author's purpose or purposes for writing this selection?
   - ☐ 3 (extremely well)
   - ☐ 2 (fairly well)
   - ☐ 1 (not well)

3. By the time you finished this selection, how many vocabulary words were you able to use correctly in sentences?
   - ☐ 3 (6–8 words)
   - ☐ 2 (3–5 words)
   - ☐ 1 (0–2 words)

4. How well were you able to help your partner or group create a sequence chain for the second part of this selection?
   - ☐ 3 (extremely well)
   - ☐ 2 (fairly well)
   - ☐ 1 (not well)

5. How well do you understand why people have searched for the treasure on Oak Island for more than 200 years?
   - ☐ 3 (extremely well)
   - ☐ 2 (fairly well)
   - ☐ 1 (not well)

Vocabulary Check

Look back at the work you did in the Vocabulary Builder. Then answer each question by circling the correct letter.

1. The platforms in the pit were all made of planks. Which phrase best describes *planks*?
   a. long, round pieces of broken pipe
   b. long, narrow pieces of metal tubing
   c. long, flat pieces of sawed wood

2. Which meaning of *furiously* best fits the context of this selection?
   a. with wild anger
   b. with energy and speed
   c. extremely violently

3. What is a synonym for *incredible*?
   a. unbelievable
   b. unacceptable
   c. both of the above

4. Which meaning of *platform* best fits the context of this selection?
   a. thick sole on a shoe
   b. plan of action
   c. level surface

5. Which phrase defines *expedition* as is it used in this selection?
   a. journey for a special purpose
   b. speedy action
   c. person or ship

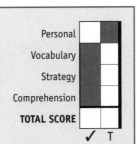

Add the numbers that you just checked to get your Personal Checklist score. Fill in your score here. Then turn to page 209 and transfer your score onto Graph 1.

Personal · Vocabulary · Strategy · Comprehension · **TOTAL SCORE** · ✓ T

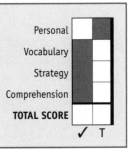

Check your answers with your teacher. Give yourself 1 point for each correct answer, and fill in your Vocabulary score here. Then turn to page 209 and transfer your score onto Graph 1.

Personal · Vocabulary · Strategy · Comprehension · **TOTAL SCORE** · ✓ T

Strategy Check

Review the sequence chain that you helped create in the Strategy Follow-up. Also review the selection if necessary. Then answer these questions:

1. Which of the following is *not* an example of signal words?

    a. since that time

    b. from somewhere

    c. nine years after the first discovery

2. What happened in 1804?

    a. A company was formed to dig down the pit.

    b. The shaft was 95 feet deep.

    c. The workers dug a second shaft nearby.

3. In what year did a drill hit a golden chain?

    a. in 1804

    b. in 1849

    b. in 1965

4. What happened when the shaft was ninety-five feet deep?

    a. Workers discovered a layer of fiber that grows only in the tropics.

    b. Workers discovered a layer of ship-waterproofing putty.

    c. Workers discovered that 60 feet of water had flooded the pit.

5. What happened in 1965?

    a. Four people were overcome by fumes and died.

    b. The businessmen and engineers ran out of money.

    c. A crew of workers finally found the buried treasure.

Comprehension Check

Review the selection if necessary. Then answer these questions:

1. Where is Oak Island?

    a. in the San Francisco Bay area

    b. in Baffin Bay, Canada

    c. in Mahone Bay, Canada

2. What led Dan McGinnis to think there was buried treasure on Oak Island?

    a. He found a pit with the remains of a pulley in the tree above it.

    b. He had been hearing stories about the treasure all his life.

    c. He found gold coins on the ground while he was exploring.

3. Why is the hole called the "money pit"?

    a. A treasure chest with money was found in it.

    b. Many people have spent all their money digging in it.

    c. People have found money hidden under all the planks.

4. How long have people been digging for the treasure of Oak Island?

    a. since 1795

    b. since 1804

    c. since 1965

5. What do you think was the author's main purpose for writing this selection?

    a. to express

    b. to inform

    c. to persuade

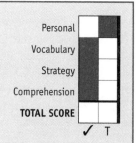

Check your answers with your teacher. Give yourself 1 point for each correct answer, and fill in your Strategy score here. Then turn to page 209 and transfer your score onto Graph 1.

Personal
Vocabulary
Strategy
Comprehension
TOTAL SCORE

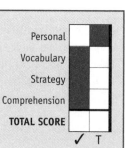

Check your answers with your teacher. Give yourself 1 point for each correct answer, and fill in your Comprehension score here. Then turn to page 209 and transfer your score onto Graph 1.

Personal
Vocabulary
Strategy
Comprehension
TOTAL SCORE

Extending

Choose one or more of these activities:

BRAINSTORM A SOLUTION TO THE WATER PROBLEM

With a partner or a small group of classmates, brainstorm some creative ways in which engineers could get rid of the water in the holes. Use information from this selection and some of the resources on this page.

CREATE A PICTURE BOOK

Part of the fun of learning new information is being able to share it with others. Create an informational picture book about Oak Island and the mysterious treasure. Some of the resources listed on this page can help you get started. Be sure to include a map that shows where Oak Island is located. Display your book in your school or classroom library so others can read it.

DESIGN A TREASURE HUNT

Treasure hunts are always a lot of fun. With a partner, draw a treasure map and hide some "treasures" for others to find. Trade your map with another pair of students, and see who can find the treasure first.

Resources

Books

Crooker, William S. *Oak Island Gold.* Nimbus Publishing, 1993.

Finnan, Mark. *Oak Island Secrets.* Formac, 2002.

Sora, Steven. *The Lost Treasure of the Knights Templar: Solving the Oak Island Mystery.* Destiny Books, 1999.

Web Site

http://www.oakislandtreasure.com/
This Web site presents information on Oak Island. It includes photographs of the island.

Raining Rocks?

Building Background

What would you do if a rock fell from the sky into your house? We've all heard about strange lights and mysterious objects falling through the sky, but how much do we really know about them?

Before you begin reading "Raining Rocks?" get together with a partner and write down at least three things that you know—or think you know—about meteors, meteorites, and meteoroids. Then list at least three questions that you have about them. When you finish the selection, you will list three things that you learned from it.

K (What I **K**now)	W (What I **W**ant to Know)	L (What I **L**earned)
1.	1.	1.
2.	2.	2.
3.	3.	3.

meteorites

meteoroids

meteors

orbits

shooting stars

Vocabulary Builder

1. The words in the margin are specialized vocabulary words. As you learned in Lesson 4, **specialized vocabulary** words are related to a particular topic in some way.

2. Before you read "Raining Rocks?" complete the sentences below with the words in the margin. Use a dictionary or other reference book if you need help.

   a. Fragments of rock that travel around the sun are called

   _____.

   b. The paths that the rocks follow around the sun are called

   _____.

   c. When meteoroids burn up in Earth's atmosphere, they are called

   _____, or _____.

   d. When meteoroids land on Earth, they are called

   _____.

3. Save your work. You will refer to it again in the Vocabulary Check.

Strategy Builder

Outlining Main Ideas and Supporting Details

- As you learned in Lesson 4, **nonfiction** is writing that gives readers information about a particular topic. The topic of this selection is "raining rocks"— meteors, meteorites, and meteoroids.

- Even though some of the events in this selection are told in sequence, the main organizational pattern of "Raining Rocks?" is **description**. Descriptions tell what things are or how they work. They usually are organized according to **main ideas** and **supporting details**.

- There are many ways to keep track of main ideas and details as you read. One way is to use a concept map. Another way is to use an outline. Some outlines use a system of Roman numerals (I, II, III, and so on), capital letters, and Arabic numerals (1, 2, 3, and so on).

- Read the following paragraph from the article "Bears." Then read how one student outlined the main ideas and details.

> Bears are usually born in the winter den of the mother. They are tiny at birth; a newborn black bear cub, for example, weighs less than a pound. But the cubs grow fast on their mother's rich milk and are ready to explore when the time comes to leave the den. Young bears depend on their mother to teach them what they need to know to survive. They learn from her how to avoid danger and where to find food.

    I. Bears

        A. Bear Cubs

            1. born in the winter

            2. tiny at birth

            3. grow fast on mother's milk

            4. learn from mother how to survive

Raining Rocks?

by Patricia Lauber

As you read the first part of this selection, apply the strategies that you just learned. Look for the main ideas and supporting details in this description, and think about how you might outline them.

On the evening of November 8, 1982, a rock the size of a grapefruit fell out of the sky above Wethersfield, Connecticut. Traveling at three hundred miles an hour, it crashed through the roof of a house, ripped through an upstairs closet, shot into the living room below, bounced sideways into the dining room, hit the ceiling, and finally came to rest under the dining-room table.

The owners of the house, Robert and Wanda Donahue, had been watching television in a room off the kitchen. Their first thought was that they had been bombed. They leaped to their feet, ran through the dining room without seeing the rock, and came to the living room. It was littered with plaster, dust, and bits of wood. The Donahues telephoned for help.

Checking the house, firemen discovered the rock. Its outside was a blackened crust, its inside light gray, as a few chipped spots showed. A fireman recognized it for what it was: a meteorite, a rock that had fallen to Earth from space.

Meteorites are rare, and it is extremely unusual for them to damage property or injure people or animals. In all of recorded history, only one person is known to have been hurt by a meteorite—a woman in Alabama, who was bruised when a nine-pound meteorite tore through the roof of her house in 1954, bounced off a radio, and hit her. Only fifteen houses are known to have been damaged by meteorites. Oddly enough, two of them were in Wethersfield. In 1971 a meteorite crashed into a house there and lodged in the living-room ceiling.

Stranger yet, the Donahues' meteorite was the third known to have hit the small state of Connecticut. The first fell on December 14, 1807, in the town of Weston.

About 6:30 that morning, while the day was still dark, Nathan Wheeler was walking through a field on his farm in northeastern Weston (now called Easton). A sudden flash lighted up everything around him. Looking up, he saw a ball of fire in the sky to the north. Elihu Staples, who lived nearby, heard three loud noises that sounded like cannon fire and saw the fireball give three leaps. A rushing sound, like a whirlwind, passed to the east of his house, and something heavy hit the ground. On a neighboring farm, terrified cattle jumped a fence, and the farmer later came on a place where the ground was torn up and littered with fragments of unfamiliar rock.

At the time, few people had heard of meteorites, and the farmers of Weston did not know what to make of this strange event—a brilliant light, explosions, and a rain of rocks. But they searched for fallen rocks, hoping these might hold gold or at least have value as souvenirs.

One person who did know about meteorites was Benjamin Silliman, a science professor at Yale College in New Haven. He had learned about them while studying in France, and when he heard of the fireball, he seized the chance to learn more. Hurrying to Weston, he spent a week interviewing everyone who might have seen the fireball and trying to collect samples of the rock for study. Later, Silliman managed to buy a 25-pound piece for Yale. He estimated that the whole meteorite must have weighed 350 pounds.

The Weston fireball was important because it was the first recorded fall of a meteorite in North America. Silliman's studies were important because they helped to prove that from time to time rocks did fall to earth out of the sky. For hundreds of years learned men had refused to believe that such a thing could happen. They scoffed at reports telling of exploding fireballs and rains of rocks. Not until the late 1700s and early 1800s did some scientists begin to believe that there were rocks in space that sometimes fell to Earth. This change of mind opened up a new field of study.

 Stop here for the Strategy Break.

Strategy Break

If you were to create an outline for this selection so far, it might look like this:

I. Meteorites in North America

   A. November 8, 1982
      1. size of a grapefruit
      2. traveled 300 mph
      3. landed under the Donahues' dining room table in Wethersfield, CT

   B. 1954
      1. Alabama
      2. nine pounds
      3. hit and injured a woman

   C. 1971
      1. Wethersfield, CT
      2. lodged in the living-room ceiling

   D. December 14, 1807
      1. Weston, CT
      2. a brilliant light, explosions, a rain of rocks
      3. whole thing must have weighed 350 pounds
      4. first recorded fall of a meteorite in N. America

As you continue reading, keep paying attention to the main ideas and supporting details. At the end of this selection you will use some of them to complete an outline of own.

 Go on reading.

Today we know that there are vast quantities of rocky objects and dust particles in the solar system. They travel around the sun in paths called **orbits**, just as the planets do. As long as these objects are in space, they are known as **meteoroids**.

Some meteoroids travel in orbits that cross the earth's orbit. If the earth and a meteoroid happen to meet at a crossing point, the meteoroid plunges into the earth's atmosphere. Traveling as fast as forty-five miles a second, the speeding meteoroid collides with molecules of air and is heated by friction, just as a returning space capsule is.

Meteoroids that glow with heat are called **meteors**. Most are no bigger than grains of sand. When they are heated, they burn up, or turn to vapor, leaving a trail of brightly glowing gases. They are seen in the night sky as streaks of brilliant light that suddenly appear and just as suddenly disappear. Although many people speak of them as falling stars or **shooting stars**, their correct name is meteors.

Sometimes meteoroids the size of your fist or bigger plunge into the atmosphere. They form the brightest meteors of all and are called fireballs. The brightest fireballs may outshine the moon or even the sun. A fireball has a brilliant, tear-shaped head and is accompanied by a trail of light and scattered sparks.

Meteoroids and meteors that survive their trip through the atmosphere and reach the Earth's surface are called meteorites.

Some meteoroids are tiny—smaller than specks of dust. They give off heat very quickly and neither glow nor burn up. Instead, they simply drift down through the atmosphere. Tons of these meteorites reach the earth's surface every day and mingle with ordinary dust.

Other meteorites are chunks of rock, metal, or rock and metal. They are the remains of fireballs, like the one over Weston in 1807. Fireballs often explode, and their pieces rain down over several square miles.

Before the meteorite hit the Donahues' house, a fireball lighted up thousands of square miles in New York State and southern New England. Police stations were flooded with calls reporting bright lights in the sky and then an explosion. One observer saw the meteor break into three bright points of light. Most of it burned up in the atmosphere, but some pieces may have fallen unseen to Earth—and one piece came to rest under a dining-room table.

That rock belonged to the Donahues, but they lent it to scientists who wanted to study it. As voyagers from space, meteorites are major clues to the history of our planet. From them, scientists learn about the birth of the solar system and the shaping of the planets.

The Donahues' meteorite turned out to be a kind of rock that is the oldest known, a kind that dates back to the time 4.6 billion years ago when the solar system was just forming. ●

Strategy Follow-up

First, get together with your partner and list at least three things that you learned while reading this selection.

Next, work alone or with your partner to complete the outline for the second part of this selection. Some of the information has been provided for you.

II. Kinds of "raining rocks"

   A. Meteoroids

      1. rocky objects and dust particles

      2.

      3.

   B.

      1.

      2.

      3.

   C.

      1.

      2.

      3.

   D.

      1.

      2.

      3.

✓Personal Checklist

Read each question and put a check (✓) in the correct box.

1. How well do you understand the information presented in this selection?
   - ☐ 3 (extremely well)
   - ☐ 2 (fairly well)
   - ☐ 1 (not well)

2. In Building Background, how well were you able to list the things you knew and the questions you had about meteors, meteorites, and meteoroids?
   - ☐ 3 (extremely well)
   - ☐ 2 (fairly well)
   - ☐ 1 (not well)

3. In the Vocabulary Builder, how many words were you able to use correctly to complete the sentences?
   - ☐ 3 (4–5 words)
   - ☐ 2 (2–3 words)
   - ☐ 1 (0–1 words)

4. How well were you able to complete the outline in the Strategy Follow-up?
   - ☐ 3 (extremely well)
   - ☐ 2 (fairly well)
   - ☐ 1 (not well)

5. How well would you be able to tell someone the differences among meteoroids, meteorites, and meteors?
   - ☐ 3 (extremely well)
   - ☐ 2 (fairly well)
   - ☐ 1 (not well)

Vocabulary Check

Look back at the work you did in the Vocabulary Builder. Then answer each question by circling the correct letter.

1. What are meteors?
   a. fiery vapor trails
   b. meteorites that become fireballs
   c. meteoroids that glow with heat

2. Which phrase best describes an orbit?
   a. path around another body in space
   b. path from the sun to the earth
   c. path that moves in small circles

3. What is a synonym for *shooting stars*?
   a. falling stars
   b. meteors
   c. both of the above

4. What are meteoroids made of?
   a. thick drops of rain
   b. fiery balls of gas
   c. rocky objects and dust particles

5. What are meteorites?
   a. meteoroids and meteors that reach earth
   b. meteoroids and meteors that stay in space
   c. meteoroids and meteors that glow with heat

Add the numbers that you just checked to get your Personal Checklist score. Fill in your score here. Then turn to page 209 and transfer your score onto Graph 1.

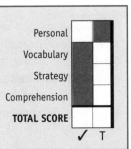

Check your answers with your teacher. Give yourself 1 point for each correct answer, and fill in your Vocabulary score here. Then turn to page 209 and transfer your score onto Graph 1.

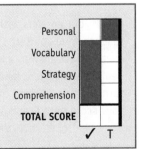

Strategy Check

Review the outline that you completed in the Strategy Follow-up. Also review the selection if necessary. Then answer these questions:

1. Which of these could be a supporting detail under "Meteoroids"?
   a. stay in space
   b. can outshine the moon
   c. fist-size or bigger

2. Under which main category would you put the detail "brightest meteors"?
   a. Meteoroids
   b. Fireballs
   c. Meteors

3. Which of these could be a supporting detail under "Meteors"?
   a. travel around the sun in paths called orbits
   b. are called falling stars or shooting stars
   c. are meteoroids and meteors that reach Earth

4. What did you write after the letter *C* on your outline?
   a. Meteors
   b. Fireballs
   c. Meteorites

5. What did you write after the letter *D* on your outline?
   a. Orbits
   b. Shooting Stars
   c. Meteorites

Comprehension Check

Review the selection if necessary. Then answer these questions:

1. Which statement is true, based on the information in this selection?
   a. Meteorites appear often, especially in Connecticut.
   b. Meteorites appear rarely and don't usually cause damage.
   c. Meteorites appear most often during the winter months.

2. Why was the Weston fireball so important?
   a. It was the third meteorite to hit Weston, Connecticut.
   b. Professor Silliman bought a 25-pound piece for Yale.
   c. It was the first recorded fall of a meteorite in North America.

3. Which word is *not* used to describe meteors and meteoroids?
   a. fireball
   b. firefly
   c. falling star

4. Which of the following statements is correct?
   a. Most meteoroids are 4.6 billion years old.
   b. Most meteoroids weigh as much as 350 pounds.
   c. Most meteoroids are no bigger than grains of sand.

5. What is *not* a reason why scientists study meteorites?
   a. Meteorites provide important clues about our planet's history.
   b. Meteorites provide new knowledge about the source of gold.
   c. Meteorites provide information about the birth of the solar system.

Check your answers with your teacher. Give yourself 1 point for each correct answer, and fill in your Strategy score here. Then turn to page 209 and transfer your score onto Graph 1.

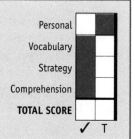

Check your answers with your teacher. Give yourself 1 point for each correct answer, and fill in your Comprehension score here. Then turn to page 209 and transfer your score onto Graph 1.

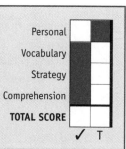

Extending

Choose one or both of these activities:

DESIGN A POSTER

Are you still having trouble keeping meteoroids, meteorites, and meteors straight? Use the information in this selection and sources listed on this page to create an illustrated poster that makes the differences clear.

RESEARCH SPACE

Work with a group to find out more about space. Use the resources listed on this page or ones you find yourself. You might want to divide your research into some of the categories below. If possible, present your findings in a multimedia presentation.

- the universe

- the solar system

- stars

- the inner planets

- the outer planets

- asteroids

Resources

Books

Aronson, Billy. *Meteors: The Truth Behind Shooting Stars.* First Book. Franklin Watts, 1996.

Gustafson, John R. *Planets, Moons, and Meteors.* The Young Stargazer's Guide to the Galaxy. Silver Burdett, 1992.

Marsh, Carole, and Arthur R. Upgren. *Asteroids, Comets, and Meteors.* Secrets of Space. Twenty-First Century Books, 1997.

Web Sites

http://liftoff.msfc.nasa.gov/
Learn about the universe and space exploration on this Web site of the Marshall Space Flight Center.

http://www.amsmeteors.org/index.html
This is the Web site of the American Meteor Society.

Arachne the Spinner

Building Background

The selection you are about to read is a myth. **Myths** are fun to read because they are stories that ancient people told to explain certain things in nature. For example, they might explain why elephants have trunks or why ostriches can't fly.

"Arachne the Spinner" is a Greek myth that explains how a certain insect came into existence. Can you predict what that insect it is?

irreverence

preened

shuttle

tapestry

transformed

Vocabulary Builder

1. Each sentence below contains a boldfaced vocabulary word. As you read each sentence, use context to figure out what the boldfaced word means. Then decide if it is used correctly or incorrectly.

2. If the boldfaced word is used correctly, write a **C** on the line. If it is used incorrectly, write an **I** on the line.

_____ a. The boy showed **irreverence** when he opened the door for his uncle.

_____ b. Sheila **preened** as she looked at herself admiringly in the mirror.

_____ c. The **shuttle** is the part of a loom that carries the thread back and forth.

_____ d. We used strong **tapestry** to seal the package before we mailed it.

_____ e. The audience gasped when the bat **transformed** into a vampire.

3. Save your work. You will refer to it again in the Vocabulary Check.

Strategy Builder

Identifying Causes and Effects in Fiction

- Many types of fiction contain cause-and-effect relationships. A **cause** tells *why* something happened. An **effect** tells *what* happened.

- To find a cause-and-effect relationship while you read, ask yourself, "What happened?" and "Why did it happen?" doing this will help you understand what has happened in the story so far. It also will help you predict what might happen next.

- As you read the following paragraphs, think about what happens and why.

> Griffin and Iza were bored and restless. "There's nothing on TV," Griffin complained.
>
> "Why don't you go out and play ball?" their dad suggested. "I'll play with you too."
>
> Iza and Griffin began to hunt for their bat, ball, and gloves. "I can't find my glove," Iza grumbled. Dad frowned and reached under the sofa.
>
> "Thanks, Dad," Iza said as she gave him a dimpled smile and grabbed her glove. Then she and Griffin raced out the door.
>
> Dad followed Griffin and Iza out the door. "When we finish playing," he said, "you two need to find a special place to put all of your sports equipment."

- If you wanted to track the causes and effects in the paragraphs above, you could put them on a **cause-and-effect chain**. It might look like this:

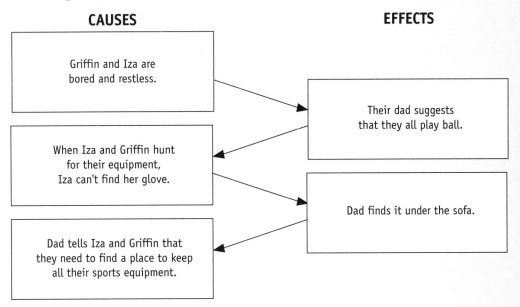

CAUSES

Griffin and Iza are bored and restless.

When Iza and Griffin hunt for their equipment, Iza can't find her glove.

Dad tells Iza and Griffin that they need to find a place to keep all their sports equipment.

EFFECTS

Their dad suggests that they all play ball.

Dad finds it under the sofa.

Arachne the Spinner

retold by Geraldine McCaughrean

As you read the first part of this myth, apply the strategies that you just learned. To find the causes and effects, keep asking yourself, "What happened?" and "Why did it happen?"

Once, when all cloths and clothes were woven by hand, there was a weaver called Arachne more skillful than all the rest. Her tapestries were so lovely that people paid a fortune to buy them. Tailors and weavers came from miles around just to watch Arachne at work on her loom. Her **shuttle** flew to and fro, and her fingers plucked the strands as if she were making music rather than cloth.

"The gods certainly gave you an amazing talent," said her friends.

"Gods? Bodkins! There's nothing the gods could teach me about weaving. I can weave better than any god or goddess."

Her friends turned rather pale. "Better not let the goddess Athene hear you say that."

"Don't care who hears it. I'm the best there is," said Arachne.

An old lady sitting behind her examined the yarns Arachne had spun that morning, feeling their delightful texture between finger and thumb. "So if there were a competition between you and the goddess Athene, you think you would win?" she said.

"She wouldn't stand a chance," said Arachne. "Not against me."

All of a sudden the old lady's gray hair began to float like smoke about her head and turn to golden light. A swish of wind blew her old coat into shreds and revealed a robe of dazzling white. She grew taller and taller until she stood head and shoulders above the crowd. There was no mistaking the beautiful gray-eyed goddess, Athene.

"Let it be so!" declared Athene. "A contest between you and me."

Arachne's friends fell on their faces in awe. But Arachne simply threaded another shuttle. And although her face was rather pale and her hands did tremble a little, she smiled and said, "A contest then. To see who is the best weaver in the world."

To and fro went the shuttles, faster than birds building a nest.

Athene wove a picture of Mount Olympus. All the gods were there: heroic, handsome, generous, clever, and kind. She wove all the creatures of creation onto her loom. And when she wove a kitten, the crowd sighed, "Aaaah!" When she wove a horse, they wanted to reach out and stroke it.

Alongside her sat Arachne, also weaving a picture of the gods.

But it was a comical picture. It showed all the silly things the gods had ever done: dressing up, squabbling, lazing about, and bragging. In fact she made them look just as foolish as ordinary folk.

But oh! when she pictured a butterfly sitting on a blade of grass, it looked as if it would fly away at any moment. When she wove a lion, the crowed shrieked and ran away in fright. Her sea shimmered and her corn waved, and her finished **tapestry** was more beautiful than nature itself.

Athene laid down her shuttle and came to look at Arachne's weaving. The crowd held its breath.

"You *are* the better weaver," said the goddess. "Your skill is matchless. Even I don't have your magic."

 Stop here for the Strategy Break.

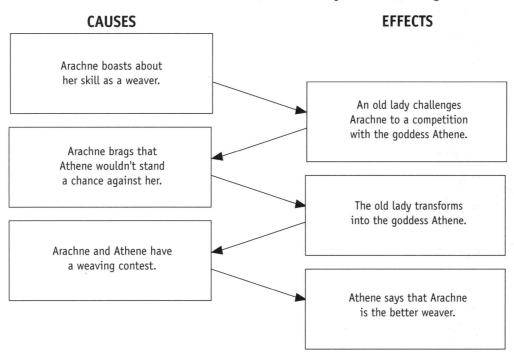

Strategy Break

If you were to create a cause-and-effect chain for this myth so far, it might look like this:

CAUSES	EFFECTS
Arachne boasts about her skill as a weaver.	An old lady challenges Arachne to a competition with the goddess Athene.
Arachne brags that Athene wouldn't stand a chance against her.	The old lady transforms into the goddess Athene.
Arachne and Athene have a weaving contest.	Athene says that Arachne is the better weaver.

As you continue reading, keep looking for causes and effects. At the end of this myth you will complete a cause-and-effect chain of your own.

Go on reading to find out what happens.

Arachne **preened** herself and grinned with smug satisfaction. "Didn't I tell you as much?"

"But your pride is even greater than your skill," said Athene. "And your **irreverence** is past all forgiving." She pointed at Arachne's tapestry. "Make fun of the gods, would you? Well, for that I'll make such an example of you that no one will ever make the same mistake again!"

She took the shuttle out of Arachne's hands and pushed it into her mouth. Then, just as Athene had changed from an old woman into her true shape, she **transformed** Arachne.

Arachne's arms stuck to her sides, and left only her long, clever fingers straining and scrabbling. Her body shrank down to a black blob no bigger than an ink blot: an end of thread still curled out of her mouth. Athene used the thread to hang Arachne up on a tree, and left her dangling there.

"Weave your tapestries forever!" said the goddess. "And however wonderful they are, people will only shudder at the sight of them and pull them to shreds."

It all came true. For Arachne had been turned into the first spider, doomed forever to spin webs in the corners of rooms, in bushes, in dark, unswept places. And though cobwebs are as lovely a piece of weaving as you'll ever see, just look how people hurry to sweep them away. ●

Strategy Follow-up

Complete this cause-and-effect chain for the second part of "Arachne the Spinner." Some of the chain has been filled in for you.

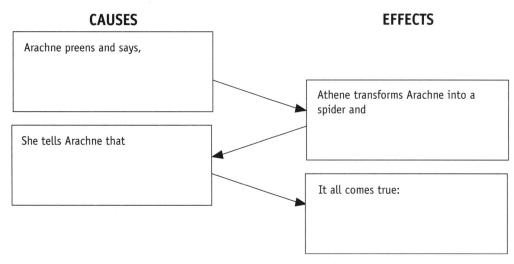

CAUSES	EFFECTS
Arachne preens and says,	
	Athene transforms Arachne into a spider and
She tells Arachne that	
	It all comes true:

✓Personal Checklist

Read each question and put a check (✓) in the correct box.

1. How well do you understand what myths explain?
   - ☐ 3 (extremely well)
   - ☐ 2 (fairly well)
   - ☐ 1 (not well)

2. How well were you able predict which insect's existence "Arachne the Spinner" explains?
   - ☐ 3 (extremely well)
   - ☐ 2 (fairly well)
   - ☐ 1 (not well)

3. In the Vocabulary Builder, how well were you able to identify which vocabulary words were used correctly or incorrectly in sentences?
   - ☐ 3 (extremely well)
   - ☐ 2 (fairly well)
   - ☐ 1 (not well)

4. How well were you able to complete the cause-and-effect chain in the Strategy Follow-up?
   - ☐ 3 (extremely well)
   - ☐ 2 (fairly well)
   - ☐ 1 (not well)

5. How well do you understand why Athene turns Arachne into a spider?
   - ☐ 3 (extremely well)
   - ☐ 2 (fairly well)
   - ☐ 1 (not well)

Vocabulary Check

Look back at the work you did in the Vocabulary Builder. Then answer each question by circling the correct letter.

1. Which of the following is an example of irreverence?
   a. being respectful toward one's elders
   b. teasing and making fun someone
   c. sending a friend a thank-you note

2. Which sentence would you *not* associate with preening?
   a. Jacob was very humble about his musical talent.
   b. Erin boasted that no one had hair as lovely as hers.
   c. Michael stood and flexed his muscles in the mirror.

3. What is a synonym for *transformed*?
   a. folded
   b. changed
   c. both of the above

4. Which phrase best describes a tapestry?
   a. fabric with pictures woven into it
   b. tape used for mailing large boxes
   c. heavy piece of carved furniture

5. Which definition of *shuttle* fits the context of this selection?
   a. spacecraft that makes short trips into space and back
   b. bus that runs back and forth over a short distance
   c. part of a loom that carries the thread back and forth

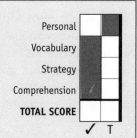

Add the numbers that you just checked to get your Personal Checklist score. Fill in your score here. Then turn to page 209 and transfer your score onto Graph 1.

Personal
Vocabulary
Strategy
Comprehension
TOTAL SCORE
✓ T

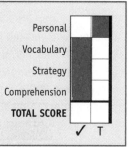

Check your answers with your teacher. Give yourself 1 point for each correct answer, and fill in your Vocabulary score here. Then turn to page 209 and transfer your score onto Graph 1.

Personal
Vocabulary
Strategy
Comprehension
TOTAL SCORE
✓ T

Strategy Check

Review the cause-and-effect chain that you completed in the Strategy Follow-up. Also review the selection if necessary. Then answer these questions:

1. What is the effect when Arachne first boasts of her skill as a weaver?

    a. An old lady challenges her to a weaving contest.

    b. An old lady transforms into the goddess Athene.

    c. Arachne and an old lady have a weaving contest.

2. What does Arachne say that causes the old woman to transform herself into Athene?

    a. She says there's nothing the gods could teach her about weaving.

    b. She says she doesn't care who hears her say she's the best.

    c. She says that Athene wouldn't stand a chance against her.

3. What is the effect of the weaving contest between Athene and Arachne?

    a. Everyone says that Athene is the winner of the contest.

    b. Arachne says that Athene is the better weaver.

    c. Athene says that Arachne is the better weaver.

4. After she wins the contest, what is the effect of Arachne's preening and boasting?

    a. Athene transforms herself back into an old lady.

    b. Athene transforms Arachne into a spider.

    c. Athene transforms Arachne into an old lady.

5. According to this myth, what causes people to sweep away cobwebs when they see them today?

    a. It is Arachne's punishment for winning.

    b. It is Arachne's punishment for losing.

    c. It is Arachne's punishment for making fun of the gods.

Comprehension Check

Review the selection if necessary. Then answer these questions:

1. Which words best describe Arachne?

    a. proud and disrespectful

    b. humble and kind

    c. shy and obedient

2. Why do you think Athene disguises herself as an old lady?

    a. She feels very comfortable as an old lady.

    b. She wants to be able to hear Arachne speak freely.

    c. She can weave better when she is an old lady.

3. Why does Athene say that Arachne's irreverence is past all forgiving?

    a. because Arachne's weaving is more beautiful than Athene's

    b. because the crowd likes Arachne's tapestry better

    c. because Arachne wove a tapestry that made fun of the gods

4. Why do you think the ancient Greeks told this myth?

    a. to explain how spiders and spider webs came into existence

    b. to warn people that too much pride can lead to their downfall

    c. to explain both of the ideas above

5. What do you think the Greek word *arachne* means today?

    a. show-off

    b. spider

    c. tapestry

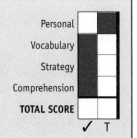

Check your answers with your teacher. Give yourself 1 point for each correct answer, and fill in your Strategy score here. Then turn to page 209 and transfer your score onto Graph 1.

Personal
Vocabulary
Strategy
Comprehension
TOTAL SCORE
✓ T

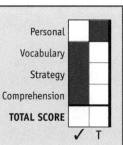

Check your answers with your teacher. Give yourself 1 point for each correct answer, and fill in your Comprehension score here. Then turn to page 209 and transfer your score onto Graph 1.

Personal
Vocabulary
Strategy
Comprehension
TOTAL SCORE
✓ T

Extending

Choose one or more of these activities:

LEARN MORE ABOUT MYTHS

Use any of the books or the Web site listed on this page to learn more about myths. Choose your favorite story, and then create a poster or storyboard that illustrates its plot. If you'd like, use your illustrations to retell the story to a group of classmates or to younger children.

PERFORM "ARACHNE THE SPINNER"

Dramatize this myth with a few of your classmates. You might want to create props, costumes, and some simple scenery for added effect. Practice your play a few times before you perform it in front of an audience.

WRITE YOUR OWN MYTH

Remember that a myth is a story that explains certain things in nature or why certain things exist. Think of something that you would like to explain. Then write a myth about it. Be sure to use a cause-and-effect chain to help you plan your myth.

Resources

Books

Ardagh, Philip. *African Myths and Legends*. Dillon Press, 1998.

Osborne, Mary Pope. *Favorite Greek Myths*. Scholastic, 1991.

Shepherd, Sandy. *Myths and Legends from Around the World*. Atheneum, 1995.

Web Site

http://www.planetozkids.com/oban/legends.htm
This Web site contains animal myths and legends.

Ruth Handler: Filling a Need

Building Background

Look around the room right now. Name the inventions that you see that fill some important needs. For example, is the room being lit by electric lightbulbs? And is the electricity that's powering those bulbs also powering a computer? phone lines? a clock? a radio? Consider these inventions, and think about what they have in common. It is the same thing that every invention has in common: it fills a particular need.

In the selection you are about to read, you will learn about the inventions of a woman named Ruth Handler. As you read, pay attention to whose needs Handler's inventions fill.

artificial

luxurious

patents

silicone

Vocabulary Builder

1. The words in the margin are from the selection you are about to read. Find those words in the statements below. If a statement is true, write a **T** on the line next to it. If a statement is false, write an **F**.

2. If you don't know any of the boldfaced words, guess at their meanings for now. Then, as you read the selection, find the words and use context to figure them out. Then go back and write a **T** or an **F** next to those sentences. Double-check your earlier work, too, and make any necessary changes.

    _____ a. The ruby looked so real that we could tell it was **artificial**.

    _____ b. The car's soft leather seats looked and felt **luxurious**.

    _____ c. **Patents** give people the right to make and sell their inventions for a certain number of years.

    _____ d. **Silicone** is a strong, solid material that is used for building homes.

3. Save your work. You will refer to it again in the Vocabulary Check.

Strategy Builder

How to Read a Biography

- The selection you are about to read is a biography. A **biography** tells the story of a real person's life, as written by someone else.

- Since the events in most biographies are told chronological order, or time order, their main organizational pattern is **sequence**. To make that sequence as clear as possible, authors often use **signal words**. Some signal words—such as *then, next,* and *a short time later*—link one smaller event to the next in a biography. However, signal words such as *When he was twelve* or *in 1886* help you see the sequence of the more major events in a person's life.

- The following paragraphs are from a biography of Abraham Lincoln. Notice how the underlined signal words help you track the sequence of events in his life. (The words signaling major events are underlined twice.)

Abraham Lincoln was born <u>in 1809</u> in Kentucky. His family moved to Indiana <u>in 1816</u>, where his mother died <u>two years later</u>.

   <u>In 1830</u> Abraham and his family moved to Illinois. <u>While he was there</u>, Abraham worked as a clerk, a postmaster, and a county surveyor. <u>Then</u> he studied law and grammar.

   <u>In 1842</u> Abraham married Mary Todd. <u>In 1860</u> he was elected President of the United States. <u>Three years later</u> he gave the Emancipation Proclamation, stating that all slaves would be free.

   <u>In 1865</u> Abraham Lincoln was shot <u>while</u> watching a play at Ford's Theater. He died <u>several hours later</u>.

- If you wanted to show the sequence of the major events described above, you could put them on a **time line**. It would look like this:

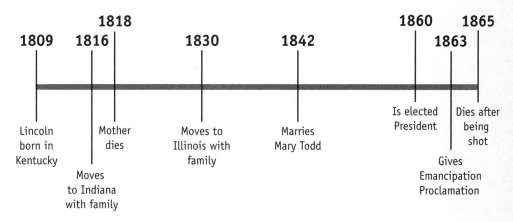

Ruth Handler: Filling a Need

by Jean F. Blashfield

As you read the first part of this biography, note the underlined dates and important events in Ruth Handler's life. (Be careful—one of the events is out of sequence.)

Ruth Handler is a woman who recognizes a need and does something about it. <u>When her daughter, Barbie, was a child in the 1940s</u>, Mrs. Handler <u>sometimes</u> watched her play with paper dolls. The flat, cardboard dolls had large wardrobes. Barbie would dress and undress them and design more clothes for them.

Mrs. Handler knew that her daughter would rather be playing with a doll that was more realistic than a flat paper one. But there was no doll on the market that had a figure like a grown-up. Instead, most dolls were round and pudgy and babyish.

Barbie Handler's way of playing with dolls stayed in her mother's mind.

The Toy Company

Ruth Handler was born in Denver, Colorado, <u>in 1916</u>. She married her high school boyfriend, Elliot Handler, and lived with him in Los Angeles, California. They had two children, Barbie and Ken.

The Handlers had a furniture-making business. The furniture makers <u>often</u> built doll house furniture with leftover scrap wood. <u>In 1946</u>, the Handlers started a toy company, the Mattel Company, to sell the toy furniture. Mattel <u>eventually</u> became the largest toy company in the world. One of the reasons it grew was Ruth Handler's doll.

Ruth Handler saw that girls like her daughter, Barbie, wanted a new kind of doll, a teenage doll with an adult figure. She sketched a beautiful doll with a slender waist, pretty hair, long legs, and joints that could be moved.

Ruth asked an artist to make and remake the figure <u>until it was just right</u>. Someone else created ways for the doll's hips, arms, and neck to bend. The doll was named Barbie, after Ruth's daughter. The people who helped Ruth create the doll also have their names on the doll's **patents**.

Popular Barbie

Barbie Doll was <u>first sold</u> <u>in 1959</u>. Mattel's advertising said, "Girls of all
ages will thrill to the fascination of her miniature wardrobe of fine-fabric
fashions: tiny zippers that really zip . . . coats with **luxurious** linings . . .
jeweled earrings and necklaces . . . and every girl can be the star."

There had never been a doll like Barbie. She was an <u>instant</u> hit with girls
everywhere and has remained so <u>ever since</u>. <u>Several years after Barbie made</u>
<u>her appearance in toy stores</u>, she got a boyfriend, Ken, named after Ruth
Handler's other child. She also has a sister, Skipper, and two friends,
Midge and Christie, an African American.

Barbie and her friends are <u>now</u> found all over the world. Some Barbie
Dolls are sold in special costumes. They wear the clothes of many nations,
just like the girls who play with them.

 Stop here for the Strategy Break.

Strategy Break

If you were to show the major events described in this biography so far, your time line
might look like this:

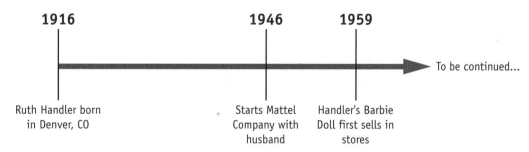

1916 Ruth Handler born in Denver, CO
1946 Starts Mattel Company with husband
1959 Handler's Barbie Doll first sells in stores

To be continued...

As you continue reading, keep paying attention to the order of events in Handler's biography.
Use the signal words to help you. At the end of this selection, you will complete the time
line on your own.

Go on reading.

Helping Women

In 1970, Ruth Handler was told that she had breast cancer. The serious, frightening illness inspired her to invent again.

The only way to treat breast cancer at that time was to remove the breast. The operation can make a woman feel a great loss, both physically and emotionally. Ruth tried to find an **artificial** breast that was both attractive and comfortable. She didn't like any of those she found.

Ruth put together a team of engineers and designers to create better artificial breasts. The designers did not just draw their ideas. They talked to and measured real women all over the country.

Finally, Ruth patented the artificial breasts under the name Nearly Me. They are made of a foam base covered by small compartments containing a thick liquid chemical called **silicone**. They feel and move as if they were real. Right breasts are different from left breasts. Like real breasts, Nearly Me artificial breasts come in many different sizes. Ruth Handler started a new company, called Ruthton, to make and sell the artificial breasts.

Today, many women, who as little girls thanked Ruth Handler for her Barbie Doll, thank the same woman for the artificial breasts she invented. She has helped them live a normal life again after cancer surgery. ●

Strategy Follow-up

Now complete the time line below with information from the second part of this biography.

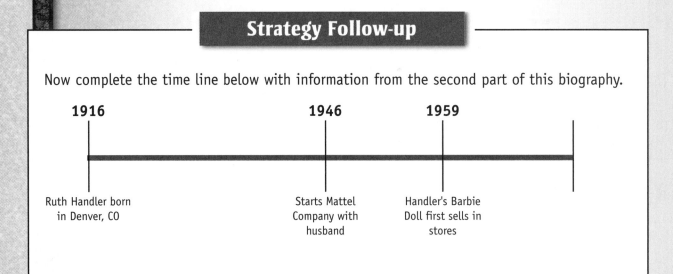

1916	1946	1959
Ruth Handler born in Denver, CO	Starts Mattel Company with husband	Handler's Barbie Doll first sells in stores

✓Personal Checklist

Read each question and put a check (✓) in the correct box.

1. How well do you understand Ruth Handler's accomplishments?
   ☐ 3 (extremely well)
   ☐ 2 (fairly well)
   ☐ 1 (not well)

2. How well do you understand why Handler invented the Barbie Doll and the artificial breasts called Nearly Me?
   ☐ 3 (extremely well)
   ☐ 2 (fairly well)
   ☐ 1 (not well)

3. How well were you able to use the information in Building Background to decide whose needs Handler's inventions fill?
   ☐ 3 (extremely well)
   ☐ 2 (fairly well)
   ☐ 1 (not well)

4. In the Vocabulary Builder, how well were you able to identify which sentences were true or false?
   ☐ 3 (extremely well)
   ☐ 2 (fairly well)
   ☐ 1 (not well)

5. How well were you able to complete the time line in the Strategy Follow-up?
   ☐ 3 (extremely well)
   ☐ 2 (fairly well)
   ☐ 1 (not well)

Vocabulary Check

Look back at the work you did in the Vocabulary Builder. Then answer each question by circling the correct letter.

1. What does the word *patent* mean in the context of this selection?
   a. shiny black leather
   b. visible or clear
   c. license from the government

2. What phrase describes the word *luxurious*?
   a. beautiful and expensive
   b. cheap and uncomfortable
   c. both of the above

3. Which method of travel would be considered most luxurious?
   a. traveling by bicycle
   b. traveling in a private jet
   c. traveling by bus

4. Which of the following sentences is true?
   a. Artificial flowers wilt and die like real flowers.
   b. Unlike real flowers, artificial flowers never die.
   c. Artificial flowers grow just like real flowers.

5. Which phrase describes silicone?
   a. thin gas vapor
   b. heavy solid material
   c. thick liquid chemical

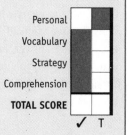

Add the numbers that you just checked to get your Personal Checklist score. Fill in your score here. Then turn to page 209 and transfer your score onto Graph 1.

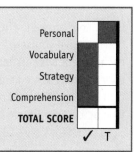

Check your answers with your teacher. Give yourself 1 point for each correct answer, and fill in your Vocabulary score here. Then turn to page 209 and transfer your score onto Graph 1.

Strategy Check

Review the time line that you completed in the Strategy Follow-up. Also review the selection. Then answer these questions:

1. How old was Ruth Handler when she and her husband started the Mattel Company?

    a. about 30

    b. about 43

    c. about 54

2. How many years passed between the time the Handlers started Mattel and the sale of the first Barbie Doll?

    a. about 30 years

    b. about 24 years

    c. about 13 years

3. Which event happened in 1959?

    a. Ruth Handler was born in Denver, Colorado.

    b. Ruth married her high school boyfriend.

    c. Ruth's Barbie Doll was first sold in stores.

4. In what year did Ruth Handler discover that she had breast cancer?

    a. 1970

    b. 1959

    c. 1946

5. Which of the following is *not* an example of signal words?

    a. in the 1940s

    b. but there was no doll

    c. after cancer surgery

Comprehension Check

Review the selection if necessary. Then answer these questions:

1. What led Ruth Handler and her husband to start the Mattel Company?

    a. It was a way for them to sell the toys that their toy makers made.

    b. It was a way to sell the toy furniture that their furniture makers made.

    c. It was a way for them to sell the games that they made up.

2. Why happened to the Mattel company?

    a. It becomes the largest toy company in the world.

    b. It began to lose money and eventually closed.

    c. It eventually became the Ruthton Company.

3. Why did Ruth Handler invent the Barbie doll?

    a. She loved dolls and wanted a new one to play with.

    b. She wanted to do something with her company's leftover plastic.

    c. She saw that girls wanted a teenage doll with an adult figure.

4. After whom are the Barbie and Ken dolls named?

    a. Ruth Handler's daughter and husband

    b. Ruth Handler's daughter and son

    c. Ruth Handler's mother and father

5. When did Handler invent the artificial breasts called Nearly Me?

    a. after she had surgery for breast cancer

    b. before she had surgery for breast cancer

    c. after her daughter had surgery for breast cancer

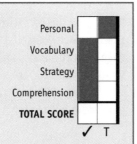

Check your answers with your teacher. Give yourself 1 point for each correct answer, and fill in your Strategy score here. Then turn to page 209 and transfer your score onto Graph 1.

Personal

Vocabulary

Strategy

Comprehension

TOTAL SCORE

✓ T

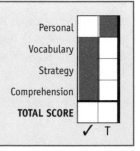

Check your answers with your teacher. Give yourself 1 point for each correct answer, and fill in your Comprehension score here. Then turn to page 209 and transfer your score onto Graph 1.

Personal

Vocabulary

Strategy

Comprehension

TOTAL SCORE

✓ T

Extending

Choose one or both of these activities:

RESEARCH THE HISTORY OF DOLL MAKING

Use some of the resources listed on this page to trace the history of doll making. You might record the major events on a time line like the one you completed in this lesson. Make sure you find out the impact that the Barbie Doll had on the history of doll making.

DESIGN YOUR OWN DOLL

Think about children growing up today. What kind of doll or dolls might they enjoy playing with? What kinds of accessories might the dolls have? Design your own doll or dolls that would fill the needs of some of today's kids. Draw or sculpt the doll or dolls, and create an advertising brochure that explains their special features and accessories.

Resources

Web Sites

http://ctdollartists.com/history.htm
This Web page offers a brief history of dolls.

http://www.marlbe.com/barbiedolls.cfm?edit_id=26
This Web site presents an article on the history of the American fashion doll. For information about the Barbie doll, click on "Part 2" near the bottom of the first article.

Team Darby (Part 1)

Building Background

Have you ever been embarrassed by something that one or both of your parents did in front of your friends? How did it make you feel? Think about that time, and then answer the following questions:

- What did your parent (or parents) do that made you embarrassed? _____
  _____
  _____

- How did your friends react? _____
  _____
  _____

- What did you do? _____
  _____
  _____

- How did things turn out? _____
  _____
  _____

In the story you are about to read, Matt Darby plans to enter his school's two-on-two parent-child basketball tournament. What do you predict might happen?

Vocabulary Builder

baffling

inconceivable

intimidate

plaintively

stature

1. Read the questions below. The boldfaced word in each question is a vocabulary word from Part 1 of "Team Darby."

2. Choose the correct answer, and write it on the line.

   a. Which person's **stature** would have the most impact on his or her profession— a dentist, a jockey, or a secretary?   _____

   b. Which animal is most likely to **intimidate** people—a lamb, a dog, or a lion?   _____

   c. Which do most people find **inconceivable**—space shuttles or UFOs?   _____

   d. If you found a math problem **baffling**, would it be confusing, frightening, or exciting?   _____

   e. If Henry described his dog's illness **plaintively**, would he be speaking happily, sadly, or angrily?   _____

3. Save your work. You will refer to it again in the Vocabulary Check.

Strategy Builder

Making Predictions While Reading a Story

- While you read, you often make predictions. As you learned in Lesson 1, a **prediction** is a kind of guess. To make a prediction, you must take the clues that the author gives you and use them to figure out what might happen next.

- As you read Part 1 of "Team Darby" you will pause twice to make predictions. At Strategy Break #1, you will write down your predictions. You also will write which clues helped you make your predictions.

- At Strategy Break #2, you will check your earlier predictions. Then you will make more predictions, and you will tell which clues helped you make them.

- After you finish reading the story, you will see if any of your predictions matched what happened in the story.

Team Darby (Part 1)

by Geof Smith

The posters were up all over school. May Madness was back.

Every spring Lincoln Junior High sponsored a two-on-two parent-child basketball tournament, and now that Matt Darby was in junior high school, he couldn't wait to enter. Most of the guys on Matt's basketball team were planning to participate in the outdoor tournament, which was slated to be held in two weeks.

Matt stood in front of the sign-up sheet, visualizing the tournament in his mind. He was positive he and his mom could win it all. They'd been playing ball together since Matt was old enough to stand. His mom had been a college player and had passed both her love of the game and her talent on to Matt. Over the years they had spent countless hours shooting hoops in the driveway. They knew each other's moves inside and out. They would be formidable contenders, Matt thought, sure as he was alive. He could practically see himself holding the trophy over his head.

"Hey, Darby," boomed a voice from behind Matt. Startled, he spun around to see Trent Walker, star of the varsity basketball team. Trent was the tallest kid in school, and he loved to use his **stature** to **intimidate** smaller students, especially new basketball players. Matt couldn't stand him. "Can't wait to stomp all over you and your dorky old man in the tournament. You think he can pry his nose away from his computer long enough to get beat?"

His father? Matt was momentarily confused. Then his eyes focused on the sign-up sheet in front of him, and for the first time he read the names already scrawled on the list: *Jim and Justin Fuller, Dave and John Carmichael, Lee and Darren Meyers. . . .* Every single student on the list had signed up with his dad. It was assumed that Matt would, too.

His heart sank.

By all accounts Matt's father was a nerd. A computer programmer, Mr. Darby spent most of his time with his face pressed up against a monitor, his thick glasses the only thing preventing his eyes from actually touching the screen. The thought of his father handling a basketball was nothing short of **inconceivable** to Matt. On the other hand, he wondered if he'd be laughed off the court for showing up with his mother. But hadn't Tim Reilly played with his mom last year? And they had done pretty well.

Another student had even played with an older sister. Nevertheless, Matt was certain Trent would never let him live it down.

Finally he took a pen from his backpack, wrote *Team Darby* on the next available line, and turned to face Trent. "I'll see you on the court."

🛑 **Stop here for Strategy Break #1.**

Strategy Break #1

1. What do you predict will happen next? _____
   _____

2. Why do you think so? _____
   _____

3. What clues from the story helped you make your prediction(s)? _____
   _____

➡️ **Go on reading to see what happens.**

By dinner that night, Matt had decided that showing up with his mother as his teammate wasn't such a big deal, regardless of what Trent Walker might say. Even Trent would shut up when he saw how tough Team Darby played. Besides, Matt concluded that it was better to go with Mom and have a chance at the trophy than to go with Dad and have no chance at all.

During dinner Matt was anxious to announce the tournament to his parents. They were involved in a conversation about the new software Mr. Darby was creating. Matt hated these talks. His dad's interest in computers and numbers was **baffling** to him. He usually tuned out and daydreamed about sports while his father droned about register overflow, fuzzy logic, unimplemented traps—stuff like that. Finally Matt cleared his throat and said, "So, the big two-on-two basketball tournament is a week from Saturday. I signed us up."

"That's great, honey," his mother said, smiling.

"That *is* great!" Mr. Darby said. "I mean, I'm not exactly Michael Jordan or anything, but with a little practice, I'm sure I could learn a thing or two."

Matt's jaw nearly touched the table.

"Anyway," Mr. Darby continued, "we'll have a great time, son, and that's the important thing, right?"

Matt couldn't believe his ears. He hadn't even mentioned anything about inviting his *dad* to play! He would have to set things straight immediately. *Sorry, Dad, but it was Mom I intended to invite to the tournament, not you!*

He looked **plaintively** at his mother, who seemed as surprised as he was. She gave him a smile and shrugged her shoulders, as if to say, *It's up to you.*

Matt turned back toward his father. Mr. Darby was holding Matt's younger sister, Lisa, on his lap, laughing. "Imagine me and Matty together on the court. Your mom will have to give me some pointers! I'll be darned. A father-son tournament!" His cheeks were glowing. He turned to face Matt and asked, "So, when do we start practice?"

"Tomorrow, Dad," Matt muttered.

 Stop here for Strategy Break #2.

Strategy Break #2

1. Do your earlier predictions match what happened? _____ Why or why not? _____
   _____

2. What do you predict will happen next? _____
   _____

3. Why do you think so? _____
   _____

4. What clues from the story helped you make your prediction(s)? _____
   _____

 Go on reading to see what happens.

What have I done? Matt asked himself all through the following day. He couldn't stop thinking about the tournament. He had been worried about showing up with his mother, but this was ten times worse. How could he get out of it? He considered faking an illness or an injury. But Mr. Darby had been so excited about playing in the tournament, Matt couldn't bring himself to back out. He moped around school and paid little attention to his classes, hoping his dad would forget about the tournament.

No such luck.

When Matt returned from school, he found his father already at home, clad in sweatpants, a sweatshirt, and . . . loafers.

"Dad, what are you doing home so early?"

"I thought I'd get home to start practicing, buddy."

Buddy? Matt's father had never called him that before. The two had a good relationship, but Matt had never considered them "buddies."

"Um, okay, just let me get changed. And do you think you could put on some sneakers? You know, so your feet don't get sore?"

"Well, I would, but it's a funny thing. I don't have any!" he grinned. Matt tried to remember ever seeing his father in workout gear before and realized he never had. *This is definitely going to be worse than I thought.*

Matt trudged upstairs to his room and took his time changing into shorts and a T-shirt. Finally he dragged himself outside to the driveway, where his father was holding a basketball awkwardly in his hands. Matt decided to go over some of the rules of the game before they got started.

"Oh, that's okay, I know *NBA Jam*," Mr. Darby said offhandedly.

"Dad, this is *not* a computer game! You have to *play*!"

"Then what should we work on first?" Mr. Darby asked.

"Dribbling, I guess, is the first thing." Matt couldn't believe he actually had to teach his dad how to *dribble* before they could move on. He thought about the other kids who would be playing in the tournament. Their dads gave *them* pointers, not the other way around. Matt groaned.

Mr. Darby began to dribble clumsily, and each time he did the ball bounced high above his waist. After a few bounces, he lost control of the ball and tried to recover it but instead swatted it off the driveway and into the bushes.

"Well, I guess that's not as easy as it looks!" He laughed. Matt didn't even crack a smile.

"No, Dad, you can't dribble so high like that. Anyone can just come in and steal the ball. You have to keep it low to the ground."

On his next attempt Mr. Darby hunched over and tried to dribble the ball lower, but it nearly popped up into his face. He jerked back. "Whoa! The darned thing almost got me!" Matt heaved an exasperated sigh.

"No, Dad! You're leaning over too far. You just have to dribble *lower*, not lean your whole body over! Look, I'll show you." Matt took the ball and dribbled it up and down the driveway a few times. "See what I mean? Now try it again."

Mr. Darby took the ball from his son and began to bounce it slowly down the driveway. "That's better, Dad. Now try looking up at me at the same time." The moment Mr. Darby took his eyes off the ball, his hand, still making a dribbling motion in the air, missed the ball entirely. *I should have known better*, Matt thought, shaking his head.

Practice continued this way for the next hour. Each time Matt tried to teach his dad something new, it turned out looking like a comedy of errors. Worse, whenever Mr. Darby looked down at the ball, his glasses would slip down his nose and he would have to readjust them. A couple of times they actually fell right off his face. *Please don't let that happen during the tournament*, Matt thought. *Stop the game! My father's glasses are on the ground. He can't see without them! They're right there: the thick, black-rimmed pair, right next to his pocket protector.*

Finally, when he was too frustrated to continue, Matt said, "Well, I guess that's enough for today, if that's okay with you."

"Actually, I think I'm getting a blister on my palm. We probably should call it a day." A *blister*? Matt thought in disgust. *This is worse than* Revenge of the Nerds! He headed up the path to the front door. Behind him, the hard leather soles of his father's loafers clicked against the pavement.

That night at dinner Matt barely touched his food. Just thinking about the tournament made his stomach churn, especially now that he'd seen his father in action. Mr. Darby was definitely more at home in front of a computer than on the basketball court.

"How did your practice go, you two?" Mrs. Darby asked.

"It was good. Matty's a great teacher. Aren't you, sport?"

Sport?

Mr. Darby scooped a spoonful of mashed potatoes onto his plate, then served some to Matt. "Us boys better eat up. We need our strength to kick some butt next Saturday!" Matt couldn't believe his ears. Hadn't Dad noticed how badly the practice had gone? Matt wanted to crawl under the table and stay there until the tournament was over. ●

Strategy Follow-up

Go back and look at the predictions that you wrote in this lesson. Do any of them match what actually happened in this story? Why or why not?

_____

_____

_____

✓Personal Checklist

Read each question and put a check (✓) in the correct box.

1. How well do you understand what has happened in "Team Darby" so far?
   - ☐ 3 (extremely well)
   - ☐ 2 (fairly well)
   - ☐ 1 (not well)

2. Think about what you wrote in Building Background. How well can you predict why Matt might be embarrassed during the tournament?
   - ☐ 3 (extremely well)
   - ☐ 2 (fairly well)
   - ☐ 1 (not well)

3. In the Vocabulary Builder, how many questions were you able to answer correctly?
   - ☐ 3 (4–5 questions)
   - ☐ 2 (2–3 questions)
   - ☐ 1 (0–1 questions)

4. At the Strategy Breaks, how well were you able to predict what would happen next?
   - ☐ 3 (extremely well)
   - ☐ 2 (fairly well)
   - ☐ 1 (not well)

5. How well do you understand why Matt doesn't insist on having his mother play in the tournament?
   - ☐ 3 (extremely well)
   - ☐ 2 (fairly well)
   - ☐ 1 (not well)

Vocabulary Check

Look back at the work you did in the Vocabulary Builder. Then answer each question by circling the correct letter.

1. Which word or phrase describes a person's stature?
   a. hair color
   b. height
   c. athletic ability

2. Which word is a synonym for *plaintively*?
   a. sadly
   b. excitedly
   c. angrily

3. Matt finds his dad's interest in computers and numbers baffling. What is another word for *baffling*?
   a. interesting
   b. exciting
   c. puzzling

4. Which word means the opposite of *inconceivable*?
   a. unlikely
   b. believable
   c. available

5. Which phrase best describes an intimidating person?
   a. someone who helps you with your homework
   b. someone who returns your lost wallet
   c. someone who threatens to get you into trouble

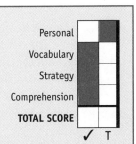

Add the numbers that you just checked to get your Personal Checklist score. Fill in your score here. Then turn to page 209 and transfer your score onto Graph 1.

Personal
Vocabulary
Strategy
Comprehension
TOTAL SCORE
✓ T

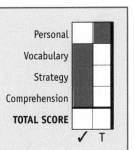

Check your answers with your teacher. Give yourself 1 point for each correct answer, and fill in your Vocabulary score here. Then turn to page 209 and transfer your score onto Graph 1.

Personal
Vocabulary
Strategy
Comprehension
TOTAL SCORE
✓ T

Strategy Check

Review what you wrote at each Strategy Break. Then answer these questions:

1. If you had predicted that Matt and his mother would play in the tournament, which clue would have best supported your prediction?

    a. Everyone had signed up with his dad.

    b. Matt and his mother had been playing together for years.

    c. "Can't wait to stomp all over you and your dorky old man."

2. If you had predicted that Matt and his father would compete in the tournament, which clue would have best supported your prediction?

    a. Tim Reilly played with his mom last year.

    b. Matt wrote *Team Darby* on the line.

    c. The thought of his father handling a basketball was inconceivable to Matt.

3. At Strategy Break #2, which prediction would have fit the story best?

    a. Matt will convince his father not to play.

    b. Mr. Darby will tell Matt that he doesn't want to play.

    c. Matt and his father will play in the tournament.

4. If you had predicted that Matt and his father would play in the tournament, which clue would *not* have supported your prediction?

    a. He hadn't even mentioned anything about inviting his *dad* to play!

    b. Sorry, Dad, but it was Mom I intended to invite, . . . not you.

    c. Mr. Darby asked, "When do we start practice?"

5. Which clue might have helped you predict Mr. Darby's basketball skills?

    a. Mr. Darby didn't even own a pair of sneakers.

    b. He could dribble a basketball as well as Matt.

    c. He and Matt had played together for years.

Comprehension Check

Review Part 1 of "Team Darby" if necessary. Then answer these questions:

1. At the beginning of the story, why is Matt looking forward to the basketball tournament?

    a. He is positive he and his mom can win it.

    b. He is positive he and his dad can win it.

    c. He can't wait to be stomped on by Trent Walker.

2. Why does everyone think that Matt's father is a nerd?

    a. He always wears sneakers and workout gear.

    b. He spends all his time working at a computer.

    c. He doesn't want to play in the tournament.

3. Which of the following does *not* describe Matt's feelings about the first practice?

    a. It turned out looking like a comedy of errors.

    b. It was worse than *Revenge of the Nerds*.

    c. It was good, and Matty was a great teacher.

4. Why does Mr. Darby think he knows how to play basketball?

    a. He knows how to play *NBA Jam*.

    b. He has been playing basketball for years.

    c. Both of the above answers are correct.

5. Why doesn't Matt insist on having his mother play in the tournament?

    a. He doesn't think that he and his mother can win it.

    b. He can see how excited his dad is about playing in it.

    c. He decides to fake an injury and not play in it at all.

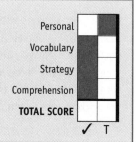

Check your answers with your teacher. Give yourself 1 point for each correct answer, and fill in your Strategy score here. Then turn to page 209 and transfer your score onto Graph 1.

Personal
Vocabulary
Strategy
Comprehension
TOTAL SCORE
✓ T

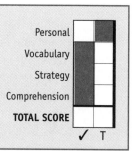

Check your answers with your teacher. Give yourself 1 point for each correct answer, and fill in your Comprehension score here. Then turn to page 209 and transfer your score onto Graph 1.

Personal
Vocabulary
Strategy
Comprehension
TOTAL SCORE
✓ T

Extending

Choose one or more of these activities:

WRITE PART 2 OF "TEAM DARBY"

Before you read Part 2 in Lesson 11, write your own ending to this story. Use the clues that the author gives to help you predict what might happen. Compare your version of "Team Darby," Part 2, with other classmates' versions. You might want to give awards for whose version is most creative, silliest, most unlikely, and so on. When you finish Lesson 11, you can give an award to the student or students whose version best matches what happens in the *real* "Team Darby," Part 2.

LEARN ABOUT HOOPS HISTORY

What do you know about the history of basketball? Who invented it? Where and why was it invented? How has it developed and changed through the years? Research the game by yourself or with a partner, and then present your findings to the class. Use one of more of the following ideas to make your presentation:

- a mural

- a time line

- pictures

- diagrams

- a scale drawing

- a diorama

READ OTHER BASKETBALL STORIES

Read other basketball stories and share your opinions of them. You and your classmates might write brief reports on 3"×5" cards. Place the cards in a file box that others can access. If you read the same book or story as someone else, add or attach your comments to his or her card.

Resources

Books

Herman, Hank. *Above the Rim.* Super Hoops. Skylark, 1997.

McKissack, Fredrick, Jr. *Black Hoops: The History of African Americans in Basketball.* Scholastic, 1999.

Myers, Walter Dean. *Hoops.* Bt Bound, 1999.

Smith, Geof. *Above 95th Street and Other Basketball Stories.* Sports Shorts. Lowell House, 1997.

Web Site

http://www.hoophall.com/history/history.htm
Click on the "James Naismith Section" of this Web site for information on the inventor of basketball.

VOCABULARY

From Lesson 8
- transformed

From Lesson 6
- incredible

Learning New Words

Prefixes

A prefix is a word part that is added to the beginning of a root word. (*Pre-* means "before.") When you add a prefix, you often change the root word's meaning and function. For example, the prefix *un-* means "not," so adding *un-* to the root word *done* changes *done* to its antonym, *undone.*

trans-

The prefix *trans-* can mean "across," "over", or "through." In Lesson 8, Athene transforms the boastful Arachne into a spider. *Transform* means "change over to another form."

Complete each sentence with one of the words below.

transcontinental   transparent   translator   transfused

1. Someone who changes a person's words into another language is called a

   _____.

2. When you can easily see through a piece of glass, that glass is

   _____.

3. When a person's blood is being removed and passed over to someone else,

   it is being _____.

4. A plane that travels across a continent is making a

   _____ flight.

in-

The prefix *in-* can mean "not" or "the opposite of." Adding *in-* to the root word *expensive* changes *expensive* to its antonym, *inexpensive.*

Write the definition of each word, as well as a synonym of the word. The first one has been done for you.

1. inactive   not active, still

2. incorrect   _____

3. inconsiderate   _____

4. inappropriate   _____

Suffixes

A suffix is a word part that is added to the end of a root word. When you add a suffix, you often change the root word's meaning and function. For example, the suffix *-less* means "without," so the root word *life* changes from a noun to an adjective meaning "without life."

-ly

The suffix *-ly* means "in a _____ way, or manner." For example, the word *plaintively* is an adverb that describes the way Mark looked at his mother in "Team Darby." The word *plaintively* means "in a plaintive (sad) way, or manner."
Write the definition of each word.

1. recklessly   _____

2. politely   _____

3. carefully   _____

4. thoughtfully   _____

5. clearly   _____

Prefixes and Suffixes

Some root words have both a prefix and a suffix added to them. In "Team Darby," the idea of Matt's father handling a basketball is inconceivable to Matt. The word *inconceivable* is made up of the root word *conceive* plus the prefix *in-* and the suffix *-able*. The prefix *in-* means "not." The root word *conceive* means "believe". The suffix *-able* means "able to be _____ed." So *inconceivable* means "not able to be believed."
Write the definition of each word.

1. inadmissable   _____

2. incalculable   _____

3. inarguable   _____

4. incomparable   _____

VOCABULARY

From Lesson 6
• furiously

From Lesson 10
• plaintively

From Lesson 10
• inconceivable

Team Darby (Part 2)

Building Background

From "Team Darby," Part 1:

That night at dinner Matt barely touched his food. Just thinking about the tournament made his stomach churn, especially now that he'd seen his father in action. Mr. Darby was definitely more at home in front of a computer than on the basketball court.

"How did your practice go, you two?" Mrs. Darby asked.

"It was good. Matty's a great teacher. Aren't you, sport?"

Sport?

Mr. Darby scooped a spoonful of mashed potatoes onto his plate, then served some to Matt. "Us boys better eat up. We need our strength to kick some butt next Saturday!" Matt couldn't believe his ears. Hadn't Dad noticed how badly the practice had gone? Matt wanted to crawl under the table and stay there until the tournament was over.

What do you predict will happen in Part 2 of this story? Why? Read on to find out if your predictions match what actually happens.

gearing up

momentary lapse

pathetic

protective

retrieve

stern

trounce

Vocabulary Builder

1. The words in Column 1 are from Part 2 of "Team Darby." Draw a line from the words in Column 1 to their definitions in Column 2. If you're not sure of any of the words, guess for now. Then check or change your answers as you find the words in the story.

2. Save your work. You will refer to it again in the Vocabulary Check.

COLUMN 1	COLUMN 2
gearing up	quick error or slip up
momentary lapse	harsh or cruel
pathetic	getting ready for
protective	taking care of
retrieve	pitiful
stern	beat or defeat
trounce	get or take back

Strategy Builder

Using Story Summaries to Make Predictions

- Sometimes when you read a long story, it helps to stop once in a while and summarize what you've read. When you **summarize**, you briefly describe who is in the story, where it is taking place, and what has happened so far.

- Summarizing helps you keep track of what is happening in a story. It also helps you predict what might happen next.

- Think back to Part 1 of "Team Darby." Here is a sample summary for it:

In Part 1 of "Team Darby" Matt is all excited about the parent-child basketball tournament at his school. He thinks that he and his mom have a great chance of winning it. But when he starts to tell his mom that he signed them up, his father thinks that Matt is talking to him. Matt doesn't want to hurt his dad's feelings, so he decides to play in the tournament with him. But Matt's dad is a computer nerd who doesn't know the first thing about basketball. As he and Matt practice for the tournament, Matt regrets his decision. He wants to crawl under the table and stay there until the tournament is over.

- Now use the summary of Part 1 to help you predict what might happen in Part 2. Don't worry if your predictions don't match what actually happens. You'll have a chance to make new ones at the Strategy Break.

I predict that in Part 2 of "Team Darby" _____

_____

_____

_____

_____

_____

Team Darby (Part 2)

by Geof Smith

The rest of the week passed in the same manner. Every evening Matt and his father practiced. And every night at dinner Mr. Darby acted as if he and Matt were longtime army buddies **gearing up** for battle. *Doesn't he get it?* Matt wondered. *We're going to make complete fools of ourselves, and he thinks this is* fun!

Matt wished the time would slow down, but the days passed quickly, and before he knew it, the tournament was only one day away. He and his father were squeezing one more practice in. Mr. Darby had finally gotten the hang of dribbling, but his shooting was a disaster. If he was lucky his shot hit the rim, but more often than not the ball flew over or under the backboard entirely.

But Matt had succeeded in teaching his father to pass effectively. He figured as long as his dad passed him the ball instead of trying to shoot it himself, they wouldn't be laughed off the court, and they might even score some points. Nevertheless, Matt hoped he'd get lucky and the tournament would be rained out. *If I'm really lucky*, he thought, *there will be an earthquake.*

There were no natural disasters. There wasn't even a cloud in the sky the morning of the tournament. Matt couldn't have been more disappointed. He dragged himself out of bed and pulled on his sweats. When he headed downstairs, he found his parents and sister already sitting at the kitchen table. His dad was just finishing what appeared to be a huge breakfast of banana pancakes, eggs, and orange juice.

"Hey, pal, better eat up before we go."

"I'm not too hungry, Dad. I'll just have some juice." Matt couldn't believe his dad was so excited. *How can he eat at a time like this?*

When the Darbys got to the school, the courts were crowded with fathers and sons warming up. Onlookers, mostly mothers and daughters, filled the bleachers. Matt and Mr. Darby blended into the group of fathers and sons, and although no one seemed to notice them, Matt felt like his dad stuck out like a sore thumb. Matt looked around at the other fathers. Most of them looked like older versions of their sons; they wore the same basketball shorts, T-shirts, and sneakers. Matt's father, on the other hand, was wearing heavy sweatpants and a matching sweatshirt, as if he feared catching a cold by exercising outdoors.

And, of course, he was wearing loafers. Mr. Darby also had tied a rubber cord to the ends of his glasses and wrapped it around his head to prevent his glasses from slipping off. All in all, Matt thought his father made a pretty **pathetic** picture. He knew it wouldn't be long before Trent Walker noticed, and he was right.

"Hey, Dweeby. Excuse me, I mean, *Darby.*" Trent seemed to appear out of nowhere. "It's really too bad you and your dad won't make it far enough for me to beat you, 'cause you're not making it past the first round." Trent walked away, laughing to himself.

Making an early exit didn't sound like a bad idea to Matt. That way he wouldn't have to drag out the embarrassment any longer than necessary, and his dad would have had the chance to play a little.

Unfortunately, and to Matt's utter amazement, they won the first game. Andy Dowd and his father made it hard for them not to win. Andy's father was a decent player, but Andy was not. He was even worse than Matt's dad. *Maybe we should swap partners,* Matt thought. *Dad and Andy can get killed, and Mr. Dowd and I can win the whole thing.*

Mr. Dowd was a big guy who seemed afraid of knocking Mr. Darby down if he touched him at all. So he barely defended him, leaving Mr. Darby open to pass the ball to Matt. Andy was no match for Matt, who darted around him to score easy layups. Team Darby won 20-14.

"We kicked butt! I knew we would! Who's the next victim?" Mr. Darby asked, ruffling Matt's hair. Mrs. Darby and Lisa gave a thumbs-up sign from the sidelines. Matt returned the gesture, a smile stretched across his face. How long was this going to last?

 Stop here for the Strategy Break.

Strategy Break

On the lines below, write a brief summary of what has happened so far in Part 2. Be sure to mention only the most important details and events.

_____

_____

_____

_____

Now write what you predict will happen next, and why.

_____

_____

_____

_____

 Go on reading to see what happens.

Trent Walker tapped Matt on the shoulder.

"My dad and I have you in the next game, so I guess we'll get to beat you after all. We'll go easy on your dad, though, in case he can't see the ball through those glasses." He looked as if he could barely keep a straight face.

"And my dad will be sure to keep score, in case your dad has trouble keeping all those confusing numbers straight," Matt said. He knew his dad's glasses looked pretty goofy, but hearing Trent make fun of them made Matt furious. It was only because his dad was so smart that—

"Hey sport! Let's get in there!" Mr. Darby interrupted Matt's thoughts.

"You know, Dad, Trent and his dad are kind of jerks. Just don't worry about it, okay?" Matt was suddenly feeling strangely **protective** of his father. The two walked onto the court to face the Walkers. Both father and son were extraordinarily tall. They looked Mr. Darby up and down and smiled at each other.

The referee blew the whistle and tossed the ball into the air. Mr. Walker easily tapped it to Trent, who broke away for a quick layup. The Darbys had barely blinked.

Matt trotted to the sideline to **retrieve** the ball and pass it in to his father. Mr. Walker was covering him closely, and Matt could not find a clean pass. Finally, he sent a bounce pass to his father's right side. Mr. Darby had to take a quick step around Mr. Walker to catch the pass, and in doing so, stepped right out of his left loafer. He stood clutching the ball to his chest, one foot bare, unsure of what to do next. The Walkers immediately burst into laughter.

"Quick, Dad, pass!" shouted Matt, eager to take advantage of the Walkers' **momentary lapse**. Mr. Darby quickly passed the ball to Matt, who sunk a perfect jump shot. "Way to go, Dad!" Matt gave his father a high five.

The Walkers toughened up after that, sinking basket after basket. Matt scored a few points, but the Walkers never eased up again on their defense, and their height made it difficult to get a shot up.

Finally Mr. Darby had the ball and couldn't get a pass off to Matt, who was being guarded by both Trent and his father. Mr. Darby looked at Matt and then eyed the basket. Matt yelled, "Pass, Dad! Pass!" Mr. Darby took a deep breath, lifted the ball over one shoulder and heaved it toward the basket. *Swish*.

Matt couldn't believe his eyes. His dad was jumping up and down, laughing and staring at the basket. "Maybe I am Michael Jordan after all!" he said as Matt approached. Matt suddenly felt terrible. He'd been so busy worrying about his father messing up the game, he hadn't even given him a chance to really play. He'd screamed at his dad to pass immediately every time he got the ball. Trent's father had been barking orders at Trent since the beginning of the game, and Matt realized that he hadn't been much easier on his dad. Even with the blisters and the sore feet, Mr. Darby had never complained. In fact, Matt realized, his dad was having the time of his life! Mr. Darby wasn't embarrassed that he couldn't play basketball as well as the other fathers. He was just enjoying his time with Matt. Suddenly winning the game wasn't so important.

The Walkers proceeded to **trounce** the Darbys 20–8. But Matt didn't care. He was here to have some fun with his dad.

After the game, Matt expected Trent to give him a hard time, as he'd been promising. But Trent was on the far side of the court receiving a **stern** lecture from his father, who apparently didn't think Trent had played as well as he should have. *It's just a game*, Matt thought. *He should lighten up!* Matt put his arm around his dad and together they strolled off the court.

That night, as the Darbys sat down to dinner, Matt left the room and returned with a large box. He placed it on the table in front of his father.

"What's this?" Mr. Darby asked.

"Just a little something I thought you could use for next time," Matt answered. "You know, if I'm going to teach you basketball and all . . ."

Mr. Darby opened the box and pulled out a pair of sparkling white basketball sneakers. ●

Strategy Follow-up

First go back and look at the predictions that you wrote in this lesson. Do any of them match what actually happened in this story? Why or why not?

Next, write a brief summary of the end of this story. Include only the most important characters, settings, and events.

_____

_____

_____

_____

_____

_____

_____

_____

_____

✓Personal Checklist

Read each question and put a check (✓) in the correct box.

1. How well were you able to predict what might happen in Part 2 of "Team Darby"?
   - ☐ 3 (extremely well)
   - ☐ 2 (fairly well)
   - ☐ 1 (not well)

2. In the Vocabulary Builder, how well were you able to match the vocabulary words and their definitions?
   - ☐ 3 (extremely well)
   - ☐ 2 (fairly well)
   - ☐ 1 (not well)

3. How well were you able to summarize Part 2 of "Team Darby"?
   - ☐ 3 (extremely well)
   - ☐ 2 (fairly well)
   - ☐ 1 (not well)

4. How well do you understand why Matt changes his mind during the game?
   - ☐ 3 (extremely well)
   - ☐ 2 (fairly well)
   - ☐ 1 (not well)

5. How well do you understand why Matt gives his father a pair of basketball sneakers?
   - ☐ 3 (extremely well)
   - ☐ 2 (fairly well)
   - ☐ 1 (not well)

Vocabulary Check

Look back at the work you did in the Vocabulary Builder. Then answer each question by circling the correct letter.

1. When the ball goes out of bounds in a basketball game, someone must retrieve it. What does it mean to *retrieve* the ball?
   a. get or take it back
   b. make a shot with it
   c. throw it across the court

2. Which word or words best describe how Matt feels toward his father when Trent Walker makes fun of him?
   a. geared up
   b. pathetic
   c. protective

3. Which meaning of *stern* best fits the context of this selection?
   a. harsh or cruel
   b. the rear part of a boat
   c. grim or dreadful

4. During a momentary lapse in play, Matt is able to make a basket. What is a momentary lapse?
   a. a humorous event
   b. a quick error or slip up
   c. quick laps around the court

5. Which words best suggest the meaning of *trounce*?
   a. *trip* and *bounce*
   b. *trample* and *pounce*
   c. *trash* and *ounce*

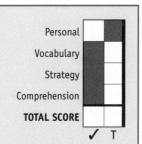

Add the numbers that you just checked to get your Personal Checklist score. Fill in your score here. Then turn to page 209 and transfer your score onto Graph 1.

Personal	
Vocabulary	
Strategy	
Comprehension	
TOTAL SCORE	

✓ T

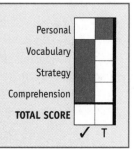

Check your answers with your teacher. Give yourself 1 point for each correct answer, and fill in your Vocabulary score here. Then turn to page 209 and transfer your score onto Graph 1.

Personal	
Vocabulary	
Strategy	
Comprehension	
TOTAL SCORE	

✓ T

Strategy Check

Review the summaries and predictions you wrote in this lesson. Then answer these questions:

1. What would *not* have been a logical prediction based on "Team Darby," Part 1?
   a. Matt and his dad will lose their very first game of the tournament.
   b. Matt and his dad will go on to win every game in the tournament.
   c. Matt's dad will do something embarrassing during the tournament.

2. If you had predicted that Matt and his father would lose the next game, which clue would have best supported your prediction?
   a. Matt's dad says, "We kicked butt! I knew we would! Who's the next victim?"
   b. When Mrs. Darby and Lisa gave a thumbs-up, Matt returns the gesture and smiles.
   c. Mr. Dowd had barely defended Mr. Darby, and Andy played worse than Matt's dad.

3. Which detail should be included in your summary?
   a. The Walkers proceed to trounce the Darbys.
   b. Matt and his father win their first game.
   c. Mr. Darby steps out of his loafer while trying to catch a pass.

4. In the Strategy Follow-up, which characters would *not* have appeared in your summary?
   a. Mr. Dowd and Andy
   b. Mr. Darby and Matt
   c. Mr. Walker and Trent

5. In the Strategy Follow-up, which important event should be included in the summary?
   a. Matt gives Mr. Darby sneakers.
   b. Matt teaches his father to pass effectively.
   c. Matt and his father win their first game.

Comprehension Check

Review Part 2 of "Team Darby" if necessary. Then answer these questions:

1. Why do you think Matt isn't very hungry on the day of the tournament?
   a. He ate a huge meal the night before.
   b. He is too nervous and upset to eat.
   c. He never eats before a big game.

2. How does Matt feel after winning the game against the Dowds?
   a. He is amazed and disappointed.
   b. He is confident and happy.
   c. He is angry and afraid.

3. After Mr. Darby makes a basket, why does Matt suddenly feel terrible?
   a. Matt wanted to be the one to make all the baskets.
   b. Matt had yelled for his dad to pass the ball, but he didn't.
   c. Matt realizes he hasn't given his dad a chance to really play.

4. Why doesn't Trent give Matt a hard time after the game?
   a. Trent thinks Matt played a great game.
   b. Trent is getting a lecture from his father.
   c. Both of the above answers are correct.

5. Why do you think Matt gives his father a pair of sneakers after the tournament?
   a. He doesn't want his father to embarrass him by wearing loafers.
   b. He thinks his father can improve his game with the right shoes.
   c. He is trying to show his father that he loves and appreciates him.

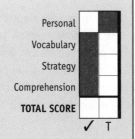

Check your answers with your teacher. Give yourself 1 point for each correct answer, and fill in your Strategy score here. Then turn to page 209 and transfer your score onto Graph 1.

Personal
Vocabulary
Strategy
Comprehension
TOTAL SCORE

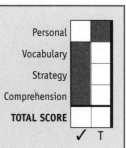

Check your answers with your teacher. Give yourself 1 point for each correct answer, and fill in your Comprehension score here. Then turn to page 209 and transfer your score onto Graph 1.

Personal
Vocabulary
Strategy
Comprehension
TOTAL SCORE

Extending

Choose one or more of these activities:

HOLD A DEBATE

At the end of this story Matt tells himself, "It's just a game." What do you think? Should people always play to win, or should they play just to enjoy themselves? Form two teams to debate this issue. At the end of the debate, have the class vote on which side presented the more convincing argument.

TAKE A POLL

With a small group of classmates, write 10 survey questions about different sports and their popularity in this country. Then have each group member ask 7–10 people to answer the questions. Combine everyone's results, and share them with the class. Which sports did everyone choose as the least and most popular?

WRITE THE NEXT EPISODE

With a partner, create another episode of "Team Darby" in which Matt and his dad do something together. For example, you might write what happens when Mr. Darby decides to coach Matt's baseball team. Or you might describe what happens when he and Matt go on a canoeing or camping trip together. If you'd like, read aloud or dramatize your story for the rest of the class.

Resources

Books

Gallo, Donald R., ed. *Ultimate Sports: Short Stories by Outstanding Writers for Young Adults.* Bantam, 1997.

Herman, Hank. *Above the Rim.* Super Hoops. Skylark, 1997.

McKissack, Fredrick, Jr. *Black Hoops: The History of African Americans in Basketball.* Scholastic, 1999.

Myers, Walter Dean. *Hoops.* Bt Bound, 1999.

Smith, Geof. *Above 95th Street and Other Basketball Stories.* Sports Shorts. Lowell House, 1997.

What's in a Name?

Building Background

What is your last name? Do you know where it came from? Do you know what it means? It may surprise you to learn that people haven't always had last names. In the article you are about to read, you will learn how several last names came about. You also will learn what some last names mean.

hereditary

immigrant

medieval

permanent

surname

Vocabulary Builder

1. The words in the margin are all from "What's in a Name?" Knowing these words will help you understand how last names developed.

2. For each word, create a word map. A map for the word *surname* has been done for you below, but you will have to use your own paper for the other ones. If you can't think of examples for each word, leave the box or boxes blank until after you have read the selection. Then add the missing example or examples.

3. Save your work. You will refer to it again in the Vocabulary Check.

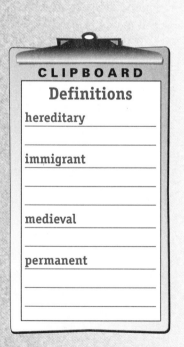

CLIPBOARD

Definitions

hereditary

immigrant

medieval

permanent

Vocabulary Word
surname

What it means
a person's last name

Example	**Example**	**Example**
Johnson	Freeman	Ming

Strategy Builder

Identifying Causes and Effects in Nonfiction

- In Lesson 8 you learned that a **cause** tells *why* something happened, and an **effect** tells *what* happened. You also learned how to find causes and effects in fiction. In this lesson, you will learn how to find causes and effects in nonfiction.

- You already know that **nonfiction** is writing that provides readers with facts and information about a particular topic. You also know that nonfictional selections follow particular **organizational patterns**, such as description, cause-effect, sequence, and compare-contrast. The organizational pattern of "What's in a Name?" is **cause-effect**.

- To find the cause-and-effect relationships in nonfiction, do the same thing that you do when you read fiction. Ask yourself, "What happened?" and "Why did it happen?"

- If you need more information about causes and effects—or about recording them on a **cause-and-effect chain**—look back at the work you did in Lesson 8.

What's in a Name?

by Martha Morss

As you read the first part of this article, apply the strategies that you just learned. To find the causes and effects, keep asking yourself, "What happened?" and "Why did it happen?"

If you've ever thumbed through a phone book, you may have wondered why we have so many different last names. Last names, or **surnames**, help us tell people apart. But surnames didn't always exist. Until about seven hundred years ago, most people had only one name—their first name.

Many American names come from England. If you had been living in England in the eleventh century, your name might simply have been William. Five or ten of the fifty people in your village might also have been named William, and it was easy to get confused.

But villagers in **medieval** England found a way to describe each person precisely. If there were four Williams in one village, one might be referred to as William, the son of John. A second might be called William from the hill. A third, William the blacksmith. And a fourth, William the brown haired.

In conversation, people began to shorten these names. They might refer to the four Williams as William John's son, William hill, William smith, and William brown.

Over three or four hundred years, these extra names gradually became **hereditary**. They were passed on from generation to generation. By the 1300s, Robert, the son of William smith, was much more likely to have the name Robert smith, even if he was not a blacksmith like his father.

As the last name became **permanent**, it was capitalized, as in William Hill. By the fifteenth century, most people of the upper and middle classes had hereditary surnames. When children took their father's last name, land and other property could be passed on more easily to the next generation.

Can you see from the above examples how surnames evolved? Names like Johnson were based on descent. A suffix meaning "son of" was added to the father's first name. Sometimes the "son" part was shortened to just *s*, as in Jones or Evans.

Names like Hill described the place where a person lived. They're the most common kind of surname. Here are some examples: Woods, Dale (valley), Knowles (small hills), Ford (shallow river crossing), and Caldwell (cold stream).

A third kind of surname was based on a person's occupation. Forester was someone who looked after the forest belonging to a rich noble. A person named Shepherd looked after sheep, and Coward looked after cows.

In the Middle Ages, more and more people began to live in towns, and occupation names such as Baker, Carpenter, and Miller became common. Over 165 names can be traced to the cloth industry alone. A person who wove the cloth might have the name Weaver or Webb or Webber. Raw cloth was beaten in water to make it thick or full. Sometimes the person who thickened the cloth trampled it in a trough, a process called walking. This is where the names Fuller and Walker come from.

The fourth type of surname was a nickname. A man named Bear might be as fierce as a bear. Someone with pale skin could have the surname White. What qualities do you think a person known as Goodman would have had?

Names are not always easy to trace to a single source. Moore, for instance, may be a placename. It could have come from the word *moor*, a wild open plain. Or it may have started as a nickname for a person who was dark like a Moor. *Moor* was a medieval name for a North African.

Have you ever wondered why some names are so common? The most common surname in the English language is Smith. Being able to work metals into tools and weapons was an important skill in medieval society, and many people were trained blacksmiths. The next most common American names are Johnson, Williams, Brown, and Jones.

 Stop here for the Strategy Break.

Strategy Break

If you were to create a cause-and-effect chain for this article so far, it might look like this:

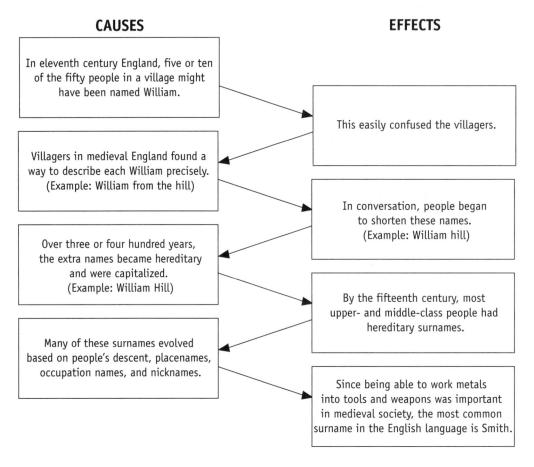

CAUSES

> In eleventh century England, five or ten of the fifty people in a village might have been named William.

> Villagers in medieval England found a way to describe each William precisely. (Example: William from the hill)

> Over three or four hundred years, the extra names became hereditary and were capitalized. (Example: William Hill)

> Many of these surnames evolved based on people's descent, placenames, occupation names, and nicknames.

EFFECTS

> This easily confused the villagers.

> In conversation, people began to shorten these names. (Example: William hill)

> By the fifteenth century, most upper- and middle-class people had hereditary surnames.

> Since being able to work metals into tools and weapons was important in medieval society, the most common surname in the English language is Smith.

As you continue reading, keep looking for causes and effects. At the end of this article you will complete a cause-and-effect chain of your own.

 Go on reading.

Of course, not all American names came from England. **Immigrants** from all over the world have come to the United States, adding new names. The most common Spanish name in America is Rodriguez. In Miami, Florida, Rodriguez is more common than Smith. It means "son of Roderigo."

Immigrants often changed their surnames when they came to this country. Many were eager to blend in with other Americans. Some of them chose American names that sounded or looked like their native names. Many Muellers and Schmidts from Germany became Millers and Smiths.

People from some European countries found that Americans had trouble spelling and pronouncing their names. So they shortened them. A Polish family named Kolodziejchuk might trim its name to Kolodzic. Paul Revere's father had a French name, Rivoire (Reev-*whah*). He said he changed it to Revere "so the bumpkins can pronounce it easier."

African-Americans also adopted new names when they came to this country. Most Africans arrived as slaves, but were able to choose their own surnames after they became free. African-Americans often picked common names such as Williams or Jones. Some chose the name Freeman.

Today some have changed their names back to African names. The poet Amiri Baraka is one. For years he had been known as LeRoi Jones. His African name means "beautiful prince."

People from China and Japan did not change their names when they came to America, but they had to spell them using the English alphabet. Some Chinese names are placenames, such as Chew (hill) and Lin (forest). But most names refer to common objects or are descriptions, such as Ng (crow), Han (fence), Chan (old), or Ming (bright). Japanese surnames usually have two parts. Toyota, for example is made up of *toyo* (plentiful) and *ta* (rice field).

The immigrants from each country have added to the rich mixture of American names until, today, there are more than a million different surnames in the United States. And as you can see, every name has a story behind it. ●

Strategy Follow-up

Work with a partner or a small group to complete this activity. Copy the cause-and-effect chain below onto a large piece of paper. Complete the chain with information from the second part of "What's in a Name?" Some of the information has been filled in for you.

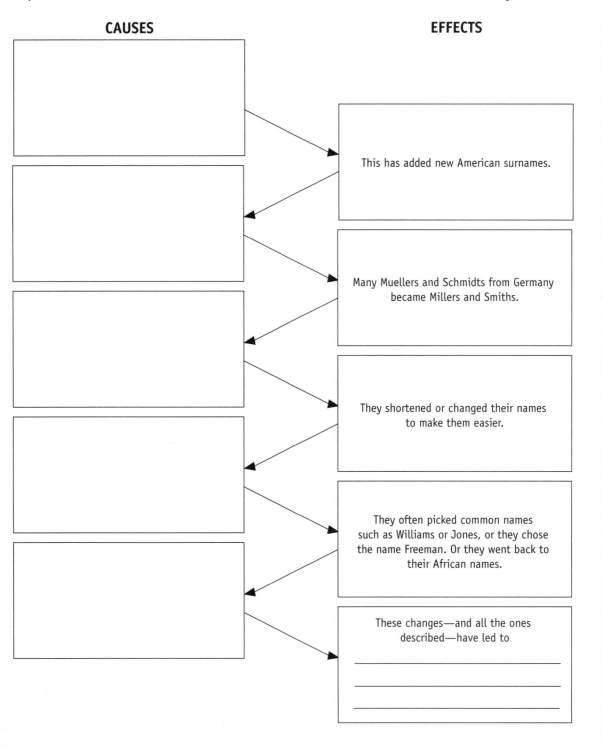

CAUSES

EFFECTS

This has added new American surnames.

Many Muellers and Schmidts from Germany became Millers and Smiths.

They shortened or changed their names to make them easier.

They often picked common names such as Williams or Jones, or they chose the name Freeman. Or they went back to their African names.

These changes—and all the ones described—have led to

_____
_____
_____

✓Personal Checklist

Read each question and put a check (✓) in the correct box.

1. How well do you understand the information presented in this article?
   - ☐ 3 (extremely well)
   - ☐ 2 (fairly well)
   - ☐ 1 (not well)

2. How well were you able to use the information in this article to figure out where your own last name came from?
   - ☐ 3 (extremely well)
   - ☐ 2 (fairly well)
   - ☐ 1 (not well)

3. By the time you finished this article, how well were you able to complete word maps for the words *medieval, hereditary, permanent,* and *immigrant*?
   - ☐ 3 (extremely well)
   - ☐ 2 (fairly well)
   - ☐ 1 (not well)

4. How well were you able to help your partner or group complete the cause-and-effect chain in the Strategy Follow-up?
   - ☐ 3 (extremely well)
   - ☐ 2 (fairly well)
   - ☐ 1 (not well)

5. How well do you understand why there are so many surnames in the United States today?
   - ☐ 3 (extremely well)
   - ☐ 2 (fairly well)
   - ☐ 1 (not well)

Vocabulary Check

Look back at the work you did in the Vocabulary Builder. Then answer each question by circling the correct letter.

1. Which of the following is *not* an example of something that is hereditary?
   a. the color of one's eyes, hair, or skin
   b. the last name of a close friend of the family
   c. land that is passed from one generation to the next

2. When something is permanent, how long is it meant to last?
   a. for a long time or forever
   b. for a few moments
   c. for several years

3. Which of the following is a person's surname?
   a. his or her first name
   b. his or her middle name
   c. his or her last name

4. What is another name for medieval times?
   a. the Middle Ages
   b. the Stone Age
   c. the Ice Age

5. Which of the following people is an immigrant?
   a. someone who was born and raised in one country
   b. someone who was born in one country and visits another
   c. someone who was born in one country but moves to another

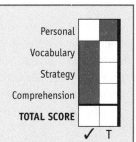

Add the numbers that you just checked to get your Personal Checklist score. Fill in your score here. Then turn to page 209 and transfer your score onto Graph 1.

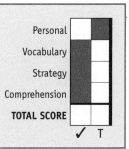

Check your answers with your teacher. Give yourself 1 point for each correct answer, and fill in your Vocabulary score here. Then turn to page 209 and transfer your score onto Graph 1.

Strategy Check

Review the cause-and-effect chain that you helped complete in the Strategy Follow-up. Then answer these questions:

1. When more and more immigrants from all over the world started coming to the United States, what was the effect?

    a. The number of surnames increased.

    b. The number of surnames decreased.

    c. The number of surnames stayed the same.

2. What caused some Muellers and Schmidts from Germany to become Millers and Smiths?

    a. They wanted to stand out.

    b. They wanted to blend in with other Americans.

    c. They wanted brand-new identities in America.

3. What did some Europeans do to make it easier for people to spell or pronounce their surnames?

    a. They said their names when they met people.

    b. They spelled their names when they met people.

    c. They shortened or changed their names.

4. What was often an effect when African-American slaves gained their freedom?

    a. They kept their same surnames.

    b. They chose new surnames.

    c. They got rid of their surnames altogether.

5. What caused people from China and Japan to change their surnames when they arrived in America?

    a. They shortened their names to make them easier to spell.

    b. They changed their names so they were easier to pronounce.

    c. They spelled their names using the English alphabet.

Comprehension Check

Review the selection if necessary. Then answer these questions:

1. From which country do many American surnames come?

    a. Africa

    b. England

    c. Japan

2. Why did people start to use surnames?

    a. to describe people who had the same first name

    b. to give people different clever nicknames

    c. to tell who got the land and property in a family

3. Why did surnames become hereditary?

    a. so a son could have the same occupation as his father

    b. because more people began to live in towns and villages

    c. so land and other property could be passed down easier

4. What does this article say is the most common kind of surname?

    a. a name that describes where people lived

    b. a name that describes what people look like

    c. a nickname that a person is given

5. How many different surnames are there in the Untied States today?

    a. more than one thousand

    b. more than ten thousand

    c. more than one million

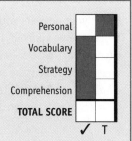

Check your answers with your teacher. Give yourself 1 point for each correct answer, and fill in your Strategy score here. Then turn to page 209 and transfer your score onto Graph 1.

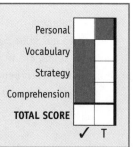

Check your answers with your teacher. Give yourself 1 point for each correct answer, and fill in your Comprehension score here. Then turn to page 209 and transfer your score onto Graph 1.

Extending

Choose one or both of these activities:

RESEARCH YOUR FAMILY'S SURNAME

Research your own family name or another surname in which you are interested. Use the information from this article and any of the sources listed on this page. Then create a family crest or coat of arms that illustrates what the surname means. Share your findings with the rest of the class.

CREATE YOUR FAMILY TREE

Research your heritage or the heritage of a famous person in whom you are interested. (If you want, it can be the same person whose surname you researched.) Use sources such as the Internet and the books listed on this page. Draw or build a family tree that shows what you have learned.

Resources

Books

Perl, Lila. *The Great Ancestor Hunt: The Fun of Finding Out Who You Are.* Scott Foresman, 1990.

Wolfman, Ira. *Do People Grow on Family Trees? Genealogy for Kids and Other Beginners.* Bt Bound, 1999.

LESSON (13) The Thief's Story

Building Background

Imagine that you are 15 years old, without a family, and without a home. You've had little schooling, which makes it difficult to find work. How do you survive?

A good story has memorable characters who capture readers' attention. In "The Thief's Story," a boy who calls himself Hari lives by his wits. A self-admitted thief, Hari tells how he survives.

bazaar

formalities

resignation

rupees

vagrants

Vocabulary Builder

1. Each question below contains a boldfaced vocabulary word. Before you read "The Thief's Story," get together with a partner and answer each question. Use a dictionary if you don't know what any of the words mean.

2. Save your work. You will use it again in the Vocabulary Check.
   a. In "The Thief's Story" the two main characters go through **formalities** when they first meet. What are some formalities that you go through when you first meet someone?
   b. Hari is always eager to make a profit of a few **rupees**. What are rupees?
   c. When looking for food or clothing, Hari always visits the local **bazaar**. What kind of place is a bazaar?
   d. Although Sara did not want to go to the ceremony, she went with **resignation**. What does it mean to do something with resignation?
   e. The police tried to get the **vagrants** off the streets. Who are vagrants, and why would they be on the streets?

Strategy Builder

Drawing Conclusions About Characters

- In fiction, **characters** reveal themselves through what they say, do, think, and feel. These clues allow readers to draw conclusions about the characters. **Conclusions** are decision that you reach after thinking about certain facts or information. For example, in the story "Mother and Daughter" you drew conclusions about Yollie and Mrs. Moreno.

- In "The Thief's Story" you will read about a character named Hari. Since Hari is the **narrator** of this story and reveals his own thoughts and feelings, the story is written in the **first-person point of view**.

- In many stories, the characters change in some way. As you read the paragraphs below, notice how Kathy changes. See if you can draw any conclusions about her based on what she says and does.

When my parents asked me to go to the animal shelter to adopt a kitten, I wouldn't go. Ever since I got scratched on the arm, I have hated cats. So my parents left me with my older sister and went to the shelter by themselves.

A while later, my mom walked into my room with a beautiful gray kitten. I wouldn't even look at it, so Mom set it down on the floor. The kitten jumped onto my lap and began to nuzzle me and purr. I slowly began to pet it. Then I found a little bell and began to play with the kitten. Finally, I couldn't help myself. I said, "I think we should call this kitten Tinkerbell, and I think she should sleep in my room."

My mother smiled. "Does that mean you don't mind that we adopted a kitten?" she asked.

- If you wanted to track the changes in Kathy's character, you could put them on a **character wheel** like the one below. Notice the conclusions that one reader drew about Kathy. They are in *italics*.

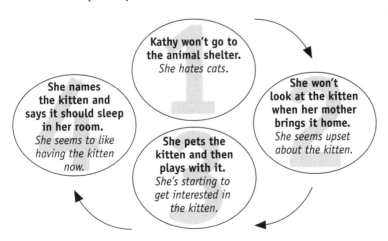

The Thief's Story

by Ruskin Bond

As you read the first part of this story, notice what Hari says, does, thinks, and feels. What conclusions can you draw about him?

I was still a thief when I met Romi. And though I was only fifteen years old, I was an experienced and fairly successful hand. Romi was watching a wrestling match when I approached him. He was about twenty-five and he looked easygoing, kind, and simple enough for my purpose. I was sure I would be able to win the young man's confidence.

"You look a bit of a wrestler yourself," I said. There's nothing like flattery to break the ice!

"So do you," he replied, which put me off for a moment because at that time I was rather thin and bony.

"Well," I said modestly, "I do wrestle a bit."

"What's your name?"

"Hari Singh," I lied. I took a new name every month, which kept me ahead of the police and former employers.

After these **formalities** Romi confined himself to commenting on the wrestlers, who were grunting, gasping, and heaving each other about. When he walked away, I followed him casually.

"Hello again," he said.

I gave him my most appealing smile. "I want to work for you," I said.

"But I can't pay you anything—not for some time, anyway."

I thought that over for a minute. Perhaps I had misjudged my man. "Can you feed me?" I asked.

"Can you cook?"

"I can cook," I lied again.

"If you can cook, then maybe I can feed you."

He took me to his room over the Delhi Sweet Shop and told me I could sleep on the balcony. But the meal I cooked that night must have been terrible because Romi gave it to a stray dog and told me to be off. But I just hung around, smiling in my most appealing way, and he couldn't help laughing.

Later, he said never mind, he'd teach me to cook. He also taught me to write my name and said he would soon teach me to write whole sentences and to add figures. I was grateful. I knew that once I could write like an educated person, there would be no limit to what I could achieve.

It was quite pleasant working for Romi. I made tea in the morning and then took my time buying the day's supplies, usually making a profit of two or three **rupees**. I think he knew I made a little money this way, but he didn't seem to mind.

Romi made money by fits and starts. He would borrow one week, lend the next. He kept worrying about his next check, but as soon as it arrived he would go out and celebrate. He wrote for the *Delhi* and *Bombay* magazines: a strange way to make a living.

One evening he came home with a small bundle of notes, saying he had just sold a book to a publisher. That night I saw him put the money in an envelope and tuck it under the mattress.

I had been working for Romi for almost a month and, apart from cheating on the shopping, had not done anything in my real line of work. I had every opportunity for doing so. I could come and go as I pleased, and Romi was the most trusting person I had ever met.

That was why it was so difficult to rob him. It was easy for me to rob a greedy man. But robbing a nice man could be a problem. And if he doesn't notice he's being robbed, then all the spice goes out of the undertaking!

Well, it's time I got down to some real work, I told myself. If I don't take the money, he'll only waste it on his so-called friends. After all, he doesn't even give me a salary.

 Stop here for the Strategy Break.

Strategy Break

What conclusions can you draw about Hari so far? If you were to begin a character wheel for him, it might look like this:

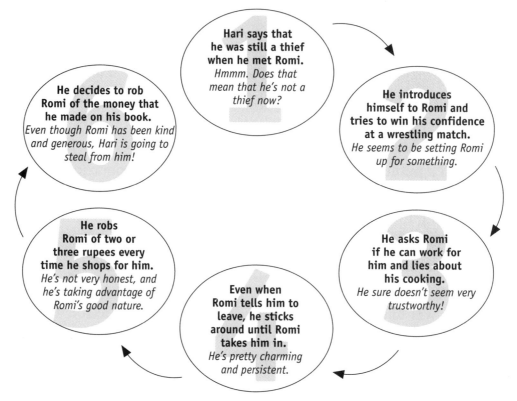

As you continue reading, keep paying attention to Hari's thoughts, words, and actions. Does he begin to change? At the end of this story, you will finish his character wheel.

 Go on reading to see what happens.

Romi was sleeping peacefully. A beam of moonlight reached over the balcony and fell on his bed. I sat on the floor, considering the situation. If I took the money, I could catch the 10:30 express to Lucknow. Slipping out of my blanket, I crept over to the bed.

My hand slid under the mattress, searching for the notes. When I found the packet, I drew it out without a sound. Romi sighed in his sleep and turned on his side. Startled, I moved quickly out of the room.

Once on the road, I began to run. I had the money stuffed into a vest pocket under my shirt. When I'd gotten some distance from Romi's place, I slowed to a walk and, taking the envelope from my pocket, counted the money. Seven hundred rupees in fifties. I could live like a prince for a week or two!

When I reached the station, I did not stop at the ticket office (I had never bought a ticket in my life) but dashed straight to the platform. The Lucknow express was just moving out. The train had still to pick up speed and I should have been able to jump into one of the compartments, but I hesitated—for some reason I can't explain—and I lost the chance to get away.

When the train had gone, I found myself standing alone on the deserted platform. I had no idea where to spend the night. I had no friends, believing that friends were more trouble than help. And I did not want to arouse curiosity by staying at one of the small hotels nearby. The only person I knew really well was the man I had robbed. Leaving the station, I walked slowly through the **bazaar**.

In my short career, I had made a study of people's faces after they had discovered the loss of their valuables. The greedy showed panic; the rich showed anger; the poor, **resignation**. But I knew that Romi's face when he discovered the theft would show only a touch of sadness—not for the loss of money, but for the loss of trust.

The night was chilly—November nights can be cold in northern India—and a shower of rain added to my discomfort. I sat down in the shelter of the clock tower. A few beggars and **vagrants** lay beside me, rolled up tight in their blankets. The clock showed midnight. I felt for the notes; they were soaked through.

Romi's money. In the morning he would probably have given me five rupees to go to the movies, but now I had it all: no more cooking meals, running to the bazaar, or learning to write sentences.

Sentences! I had forgotten about them in the excitement of the theft. Writing complete sentences, I knew, could one day bring me more than a few hundred rupees. It was a simple matter to steal. But to be a really big man, a clever and respected man, was something else. I should go back to Romi, I told myself, if only to learn to read and write.

I hurried back to the room feeling very nervous, for it is much easier to steal something than to return it undetected.

I opened the door quietly, then stood in the doorway in clouded moonlight. Romi was still asleep. I crept to the head of the bed, and my hand came up with the packet of notes. I felt his breath on my hand. I remained still for a few moments. Then my fingers found the edge of the mattress, and I slipped the money beneath it.

I awoke late the next morning to find that Romi had already made the tea. He stretched out a hand to me. There was a fifty-rupee note between his fingers. My heart sank.

"I made some money yesterday," he said. "Now I'll be able to pay you regularly."

My spirits rose. But when I took the note, I noticed that it was still wet from the night's rain. So he knew what I'd done. But neither his lips nor his eyes revealed anything.

"Today we'll start writing sentences," he said.

I smiled at Romi in my most appealing way. And the smile came by itself, without any effort. ●

Strategy Follow-up

Work on this activity with a partner or a group of classmates. First, on a large piece of paper, draw a character wheel with 11 ovals. Use the information in the Strategy Break to fill in the first 6 ovals. Then use the second part of the story to complete ovals 7–11. Some information is provided below.

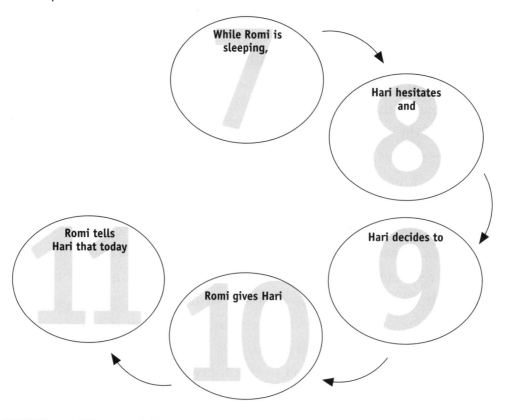

While Romi is sleeping, 7

Hari hesitates and 8

Hari decides to 9

Romi gives Hari 10

Romi tells Hari that today 11

✓Personal Checklist

Read each question and put a check (✓) in the correct box.

1. How well were you able to use the information in Building Background to understand what Hari does in this story, and why?
   - ☐ 3 (extremely well)
   - ☐ 2 (fairly well)
   - ☐ 1 (not well)

2. In the Vocabulary Builder, how many questions were you and your partner able to answer correctly?
   - ☐ 3 (all 4 questions)
   - ☐ 2 (2–3 questions)
   - ☐ 1 (0–1 questions)

3. How well were you able to help complete the character wheel in the Strategy Follow-up?
   - ☐ 3 (extremely well)
   - ☐ 2 (fairly well)
   - ☐ 1 (not well)

4. How well do you understand why Romi never says anything to Hari about his stealing?
   - ☐ 3 (extremely well)
   - ☐ 2 (fairly well)
   - ☐ 1 (not well)

5. How well do you understand why Hari returns the money from Romi's book sale?
   - ☐ 3 (extremely well)
   - ☐ 2 (fairly well)
   - ☐ 1 (not well)

Vocabulary Check

Look back at the work you did in the Vocabulary Builder. Then answer each question by circling the correct letter.

1. Which phrase below describes the word *rupees*?
   a. Indian money
   b. Indian clothing
   c. Indian food

2. In the context of this story, what does the word *resignation* mean?
   a. a written statement of plans to leave a job
   b. a giving up or giving in without complaining
   c. a feeling of patience about a situation

3. Which phrase best describes a vagrant?
   a. a train conductor
   b. a shop owner
   c. a homeless person

4. Hari goes to the bazaar to shop for Romi. Which phrase best describes a bazaar?
   a. a marketplace where many things are sold
   b. a strip mall of stores on a busy city street
   c. an indoor shopping mall with many stores

5. Which vocabulary word were you able to figure out by using the context clues "What's your name?"
   a. formalities
   b. resignation
   c. vagrants

Add the numbers that you just checked to get your Personal Checklist score. Fill in your score here. Then turn to page 209 and transfer your score onto Graph 1.

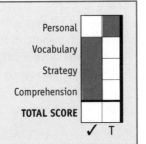

Check your answers with your teacher. Give yourself 1 point for each correct answer, and fill in your Vocabulary score here. Then turn to page 209 and transfer your score onto Graph 1.

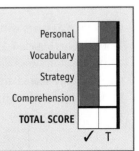

Strategy Check

Review the character wheel that you helped create in the Strategy Follow-up. Also review the story if necessary. Then answer these questions:

1. How does Hari feel about Romi at the beginning of this story?
   a. He wants to take advantage of Romi.
   b. He wants to get to know Romi better.
   c. He wants to borrow money from Romi.

2. Which of Hari's actions led you to believe that he was changing his mind about Romi?
   a. He robs Romi of two or three rupees every time he shops for him.
   b. He decides to rob Romi of the money that he got for his book.
   c. He hesitates and doesn't jump onto the train with Romi's money.

3. Why does Hari decide to give back the money and learn to read and write?
   a. He realizes it's more important to be clever and respected than to steal.
   b. He realizes that Romi will get the police after him and he'll get caught.
   c. He realizes that if he can read and write, he'll know what he's stealing.

4. How does Hari feel about Romi by the end of the story?
   a. Hari is angry with Romi.
   b. Hari is grateful to Romi.
   c. Hari's feelings haven't changed.

5. How has Hari changed by the end of this story?
   a. At first he was clever and respected, but now he is a thief.
   b. At first he was a thief, but now he wants to be clever and respected.
   c. At first he was a thief, but now he is a writer.

Comprehension Check

Review the story if necessary. Then answer these questions:

1. Where does this story take place?
   a. in China
   b. in England
   c. in India

2. What conclusion did the first sentence of this story help you draw about Hari right away?
   a. That he is no longer a thief.
   b. That he might still be a thief.
   c. That he is proud of being a thief.

3. Why do you think Hari wants to work for Romi?
   a. because he wants to steal from Romi
   b. because he wants to get in off the streets
   c. both of the above

4. Why do you think Hari misses the train?
   a. because he doesn't have time to buy a ticket
   b. because he doesn't want to lose Romi's trust
   c. because he doesn't know where to spend the night

5. Which words best describe Romi's character?
   a. generous and trusting
   b selfish and foolish
   c. both of the above

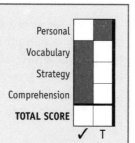

Check your answers with your teacher. Give yourself 1 point for each correct answer, and fill in your Strategy score here. Then turn to page 209 and transfer your score onto Graph 1.

Personal
Vocabulary
Strategy
Comprehension
TOTAL SCORE
✓ T

Check your answers with your teacher. Give yourself 1 point for each correct answer, and fill in your Comprehension score here. Then turn to page 209 and transfer your score onto Graph 1.

Personal
Vocabulary
Strategy
Comprehension
TOTAL SCORE
✓ T

Extending

Choose one or both of these activities:

WRITE A JOURNAL ENTRY

You read Hari's thoughts and feelings in this story. Now consider what Romi was thinking and feeling. Imagine you are Romi. Write journal entries for the day you meet Hari, the day you start teaching Hari to read, and the day you wake up and realize that Hari has stolen and returned your money. If you'd like, share your journal entries with a partner.

PLAN A BAZAAR

Using some of the resources on this page, research what you might find in a typical Indian bazaar. Then draw a diagram or build a model that shows what the bazaar might look like. Be sure to label the different booths to tell what each one sells. Display your work after you explain it to the class.

Resources

Books

Hermes, Jules M. *The Children of India*. The World's Children. Carolrhoda, 1993.

Staples, Suzanne Fisher. *Shabanu: Daughter of the Wind*. Random House, 1991.

Web Sites

http://www.mtdcindia.com/cities/shopping.html
This site describes the Chor Bazaar, a famous bazaar in the Indian city of Mumbai (Bombay).

http://www.tulane.edu/~rouxbee/kids99/india.html
This Web Site contains information on the children of India.

Left-handers in a Right-handed World

Building Background

Are you left-handed or right-handed? Or do you use both hands equally well? If you're a lefty, the authors of this article feel that you're a member of an "oppressed minority." What do you think they mean by that statement? As you read "Left-handers in a Right-handed World," see if you can discover their meaning.

adroit

ambidextrous

dexterity

gauche

sinister

Vocabulary Builder

1. Before you begin reading this article, read the vocabulary words in the margin. All of the words originally come from French, Latin, or Old English words meaning "left" or "right."

2. As you match each word in Column 1 to its definition in Column 2, think about whether the word relates to "left" or "right." Then write **L** or **R** next to the word. If you're not sure, guess for now. You can change your answers as you find the words and their meanings in the article.

COLUMN 1	COLUMN 2
_____ adroit	awkward
_____ ambidextrous	skillfulness, especially with the hands
_____ dexterity	evil and threatening
_____ gauche	clever or skillful
_____ sinister	equally skillful with both hands

3. Save your work. You will use it again in the Vocabulary Check.

Strategy Builder

Comparing and Contrasting While You Read

- Authors often compare and contrast things (and people and ideas) when they write. **Comparing** means telling how two or more things are alike. **Contrasting** means telling how two or more things are different.

- Read the following passage. It compares and contrasts two students named William and Melissa.

William and Melissa are both middle-school students. They are good friends, but they like different things. For example, William's favorite classes are biology, science, and band. Melissa's favorite classes are math, English, and art. Melissa is active in several sports, including swimming, soccer, and basketball. William plays baseball and hockey. Both Melissa and William belong to the same computer club. They also joined a new club together called Students Against Drunk Driving, or SADD.

- If you wanted to show how William and Melissa are alike and different, you could create a **comparison chart**. It would look like this:

	William	Melissa
favorite classes	biology science band	math English art
sports	baseball hockey	swimming soccer basketball
clubs	computer club SADD	computer club SADD

Left-handers in a Right-handed World

by Dr. Alvin Silverstein and Virginia B. Silverstein

As you read this article, apply the strategies that you just learned. Ask yourself how life is the same and different for left-handers and right-handers.

Minority groups have been making headlines for years, seeking and winning rights long denied them. A great deal of progress has been made toward providing equal opportunities for all people, blacks and whites, men and women.

But there is another "oppressed minority" that has not been getting the headlines: left-handers. Their group is not a small one. About one person in every ten is left-handed—at least 20 million in the United States alone. There are no laws preventing left-handers from voting or holding jobs or eating or living where they wish. The discrimination against them is of a different kind. They live in a world where common articles and tools—from desks to can openers—are made for the needs and convenience of the right-handed majority. Left-handers must make a special effort to adapt as they learn to do such everyday tasks as writing, cutting with scissors, or winding a watch. Often there is no one to give them the special teaching that would make the adjustment easier; right-handers are usually quite unaware of the left-hander's problems, and the results often strike them as awkward, peculiar, or comical.

 Stop here for the Strategy Break.

Strategy Break

If you were to begin a comparison chart for this article so far, it might look like this:

	left-handers	right-handers
number of people in the world	1 person in every 10	9 people in every 10
discriminating laws against them	none	none
common articles and tools made for them	few	most
ability to do everyday tasks	awkward and difficult	much easier

As you read the second part of this article, look for other ways in which life is the same and different for left-handers and right-handers. In the Strategy Follow-up, you will complete a comparison chart of your own.

 Go on reading.

Even our language is slanted against left-handers. The word *right* refers to the right side of the body, but it can also mean "proper" or "correct." Standing up for your *rights* means seeking justice—no one is striving for "civil lefts!" English has also borrowed some words meaning "right" from other languages, and they all have positive meanings. ***Dexterity***, or skillfulness, comes from the Latin word for "right," *dexter*. A person who can do things well with both hands is called **ambidextrous**, implying that both hands are "right hands"—an indication of how much people think left hands are worth! The French word for "right," *droit*, has given us another synonym for skillful or clever: ***adroit***.

There is nothing positive about *left*. It comes from an Old English word meaning "weak" or "worthless." A "left-handed marriage" referred to one that was not really quite legal, so that the children of such a marriage could not inherit. A "left-handed compliment" is really an insult. If you say something is "out in left field," you mean that it really does not have much to do with the subject. The Latin word for "left," *sinister*, has come into our language with a meaning of "evil" and "threatening." The word *gauche*, which means "left" in French, is used in English to mean "awkward."

Why is it that nearly everyone uses one hand more than the other and does things more skillfully with one hand than the other? Why are most people right-handed—and why are some people left-handed? Are left-handers different from right-handers? Are they more intelligent, skillful, creative, and independent? Or are they less so? Can people change their handedness successfully—and should they? Through the centuries, people have had many ideas about left-handedness. Sometimes it has been linked with magic and prophecy. Some peoples have tried to outlaw left-handedness completely. Today's brain researchers are conducting some fascinating experiments on the left and right halves of the brain and how they affect handedness. The scientists are finding answers—and more questions. ●

Strategy Follow-up

Now complete the comparison chart for the second part of this article. Use a separate sheet of paper if you need to. Go back and skim the article for information as necessary.

	left-handers	right-handers
words with positive meanings		**right** ("proper" or "correct")
words with negative meanings	**left** ("weak" or "worthless")	

✓Personal Checklist

Read each question and put a check (✓) in the correct box.

1. How well do you understand the information presented in this article?
   - ☐ 3 (extremely well)
   - ☐ 2 (fairly well)
   - ☐ 1 (not well)

2. Now that you've read the article, how well do you understand why the authors call left-handers an "oppressed minority"?
   - ☐ 3 (extremely well)
   - ☐ 2 (fairly well)
   - ☐ 1 (not well)

3. How well were you able to complete the activities in the Vocabulary Builder?
   - ☐ 3 (extremely well)
   - ☐ 2 (fairly well)
   - ☐ 1 (not well)

4. How well were you able to complete the comparison chart in the Strategy Follow-up?
   - ☐ 3 (extremely well)
   - ☐ 2 (fairly well)
   - ☐ 1 (not well)

5. How well do you understand how our language is slanted against left-handers?
   - ☐ 3 (extremely well)
   - ☐ 2 (fairly well)
   - ☐ 1 (not well)

Vocabulary Check

Look back at the work you did in the Vocabulary Builder. Then answer each question by circling the correct letter.

1. When a person is ambidextrous, with which hand or hands is the person skillful?
   a. the left hand
   b. the right hand
   c. both hands

2. Which vocabulary words mean "left" in French and Latin?
   a. *gauche* and *sinister*
   b. *adroit* and *ambidextrous*
   c. *dexterity* and *sinister*

3. Which vocabulary words mean "right" in French and Latin?
   a. *gauche* and *ambidextrous*
   b. *adroit* and *dexterity*
   c. *gauche* and *sinister*

4. What is *not* an example of someone who is adroit?
   a. a skier moving gracefully down a hill
   b. a basketball player making a perfect layup
   c. a football player fumbling the ball

5. Which activity requires special dexterity in one's hands?
   a. playing a lively song on the piano
   b. jumping rope while others twirl it
   c. running through tires during football practice

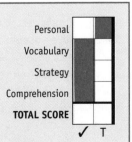

Add the numbers that you just checked to get your Personal Checklist score. Fill in your score here. Then turn to page 209 and transfer your score onto Graph 1.

	Personal	
	Vocabulary	
	Strategy	
	Comprehension	
	TOTAL SCORE	
	✓ T	

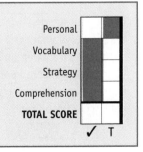

Check your answers with your teacher. Give yourself 1 point for each correct answer, and fill in your Vocabulary score here. Then turn to page 209 and transfer your score onto Graph 1.

	Personal	
	Vocabulary	
	Strategy	
	Comprehension	
	TOTAL SCORE	
	✓ T	

Strategy Check

Review the comparison charts for both parts of this selection. Then use them answer these questions:

1. How many people in the world are right-handed?
   a. 9 people in every 10
   b. 1 person in every 10
   c. 5 people in every 10

2. Which group has the most trouble using common articles and tools?
   a. ambidextrous people
   b. right-handers
   c. left-handers

3. According to the article, how many words meaning "left" are positive?
   a. none
   b. five
   c. six

4. According to the article, how many words meaning "right" are negative?
   a. six
   b. five
   c. none

5. What is the meaning of the word *left*?
   a. "proper" and "correct"
   b. "weak" or "worthless"
   c. "skillful" or "clever"

Comprehension Check

Review the article if necessary. Then answer these questions:

1. Why do the authors call left-handers an "oppressed minority"?
   a. because at least 20 million people in the U.S. are left-handed
   b. because one person in every 10 is left-handed
   c. because most common articles and tools are made for right-handers

2. What is a typical problem that left-handers face in a right-handed world?
   a. trying to cut with a steak knife
   b. trying to cut with a scissors
   c. trying to swing a baseball bat

3. Why do the authors think that our language is slanted against left-handers?
   a. because most of the words meaning "left" have negative meanings
   b. because most of the words meaning "left" are Latin words
   c. because most of the words meaning "left" are difficult to spell

4. What is *not* a question that scientists are trying to answer about handedness?
   a. Do left-handers have better senses of humor?
   b. Can people change their handedness successfully?
   c. Why are most people right-handed?

5. What is one of the ideas that people have had in the past about left-handedness?
   a. Left-handedness is linked to gender.
   b. Left-handedness is linked to eye and hair color.
   c. Left-handedness is linked to magic and prophecy.

Check your answers with your teacher. Give yourself 1 point for each correct answer, and fill in your Strategy score here. Then turn to page 209 and transfer your score onto Graph 1.

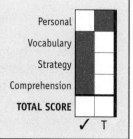

Personal
Vocabulary
Strategy
Comprehension
TOTAL SCORE

Check your answers with your teacher. Give yourself 1 point for each correct answer, and fill in your Comprehension score here. Then turn to page 209 and transfer your score onto Graph 1.

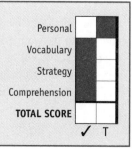

Personal
Vocabulary
Strategy
Comprehension
TOTAL SCORE

Extending

Choose one or both of these activities:

MAKE A LEFT/RIGHT DICTIONARY

Use the information in this article and sources listed on this page to make a dictionary of words that mean "left" and "right." Wherever possible, include pictures to help illustrate the words.

RESEARCH THE ORIGINS OF OTHER WORDS

The history of words and their origins can be fascinating. Choose some words or phrases whose origins you would like to know. Then use a dictionary, the Internet, and other sources to find the origins of your chosen words and phrases.

Resources

Books

Macrone, Michael. *Brush Up Your Shakespeare: An Infectious Tour Through the Most Famous and Quotable Words and Phrases from the Bard.* HarperResource, 2000.

Singer, Beth Wolfensberger. *Lefty: A Handbook for Left-Handed Kids.* Penguin USA, 1997.

Web Sites

http://phrases.shu.ac.uk/meanings/index.html
On this Web site, you can look up the meanings and origins of phrases, sayings, and proverbs.

http://www.etymonline.com/
This is an online dictionary of word origins.

Five Words

Building Background

The story you are about to read is fiction, but it is based on the true stories of many Holocaust survivors. The story takes place in Israel after World War II, which ended in 1945.

What do you know about the Holocaust? Get together with a few of your classmates and share information. Have one person in the group take notes on your discussion. Then use the notes to help you predict what might happen in this story.

anti-Semitism

Auschwitz

Holocaust

kibbutz

Warsaw ghetto

Vocabulary Builder

1. All of the words in the margin are related to the Holocaust. Use them to complete the word map below.

2. If you don't know any of the words, look them up in a dictionary or an encyclopedia. Then, as you find them in the story, you can double-check your word map.

3. Save your work. You will use it again in the Vocabulary Check.

What is one thing that led to the Holocaust?

Where were Jews sent during the Holocaust?

Where did some Jews live after the Holocaust?

THE HOLOCAUST

Strategy Builder

Drawing Conclusions About Characters

- As you learned in Lesson 13, **characters** in stories reveal themselves through what they say, do, think, and feel. These clues allow you to draw conclusions about the characters. **Conclusions** are decisions that you reach after thinking about certain facts or information. For example, in "The Thief's Story" you drew conclusions about Hari.

- In "Five Words" you will read about a character named Nettie. Since Nettie is the **narrator** of this story and reveals her own thoughts and feelings, we say that the story is written in the **first-person point of view**.

- As you learned when you read about Hari in "The Thief's Story," the characters in stories often change in some way. As you read "Five Words," pay attention to how Nettie changes as she struggles to deal with her past.

Five Words

by Pnina Kass

As you read the first part of this story, notice what Nettie says, does, thinks, and feels. What conclusions can you draw about her?

More than forty years have passed since the horrible events that are the background to Nettie's story. World War II was fought in Asia, Africa, and Europe. Almost sixty nations were part of the war, and more than twenty-five million civilians were killed. Six million of these were Jews.

*By 1941, Adolf Hitler, leader of Germany and the head of the Nazi party, had decided to kill all the Jews in Europe. Hatred of the Jews—**anti-Semitism**—became the official policy of the German government. As the Nazis invaded Europe, they arrested the Jews and sent them to concentration camps. The most horrible of these death camps was **Auschwitz**. Here, trains arrived from every part of Europe, bringing Jews to their death.*

Nettie's story is the story of many Jewish children, whose parents gave them to strangers or threw them off the death trains—anything to save them. In 1945, at the end of the war, some of these children were found by relatives and taken to live in many different countries.

There are different kinds of secrets. There's the kind you're dying to tell if someone will just keep asking you, and there's the kind that's so scary that no matter how many times someone asks, you'll never tell. And then there's my kind of secret. That's the one that's so deep inside that you don't even know it's there until something happens.

It was a warm spring day. I sat on the window sill in my classroom, watching all the preparations for the **Holocaust** Memorial Day. The sounds of the chorus rehearsal drifted up the stairs. David and Mickey were arranging photographs of the **Warsaw ghetto**, and Naomi and Judith were pinning up maps showing the towns and cities where Jews had lived. Danny stuck his head into the room.

"Nettie, instead of just sitting there, you could help."

"And what if I don't want to?" I answered back.

"Then maybe you shouldn't be part of this class!" he snapped.

Naomi dropped the map and walked over to the doorway. She whispered in Danny's ear, and he nodded slowly and went back outside. Naomi came over to me.

"Nettie, it's O.K. Don't pay any attention to him. He just didn't know."

I swung down from the sill. "I really don't know why you think you have to explain about me to everyone!"

"But, Nettie, I didn't mean . . ." Naomi looked as if I had slapped her, but I couldn't stop.

"That's right, no one ever means anything, and that's why everyone in this school feels sorry for me!" I turned around and ran out of the classroom and down the long hall. As I pushed open the school's heavy wooden door, I nearly ran into Mrs. Levy, the principal.

"Nettie, where are you running to? What's happened?"

I didn't answer. I just kept on running until I reached the duck pond. I threw myself on the bank, punching my fists into the wet grass. I felt so alone. That same feeling that I had on Saturday nights when there was folk dancing in the **kibbutz** social hall. Everybody spinning in fast circles with their hands joined and I could never catch anyone's hand. Then someone would see me and say, "Stop, let Nettie in." And then I felt lonelier than ever.

I looked across the pond. There was Griselda leading her goslings into the water for their swimming lesson. I had named her after a beautiful queen in my book of fairy tales. She was graceful and strong and a perfect mother. She back-paddled, nudging the goslings into line and making sure they weren't caught in the reeds.

I moved from the grassy bank to the shade of a eucalyptus tree, leaning back against the broad trunk and stretching out my legs. Suddenly I could remember being dragged through snow with my legs out in front of me and later someone rubbing my legs on the floor of a small house. Sometime, somewhere, long ago. And then the memory was gone. Where had it come from? On the other side of the pond, Griselda was clucking stories to the goslings clustered around her. I shivered with cold.

Past the grove of eucalyptus trees, I saw the small houses of the kibbutz, shuttered from the afternoon sun. One of those houses, tiny from here, was my house. That is, it was Uncle Max and Aunt Sara's house. Uncle Max had found me in Vienna after the war. They told me over and over again, "Now this is *your* house."

I stood up, picking the twigs and grass out of my hair. I pulled it to one side, looping the hair into a thick braid. Again, for just a second, I could see the past—my mother stood beside me, braiding her hair. "No!" I shouted. "You can't be here now. You left me!" I was sure my heart would break through my skin, it was beating so hard. I started running across the fields and didn't stop until I was home. The house was silent. A note fluttered on the kitchen table. *Nettie—We'll be back in an hour.*

 Stop here for the Strategy Break.

Strategy Break

What conclusions can you draw about Nettie so far? If you were to begin a character wheel for her, it might look like this:

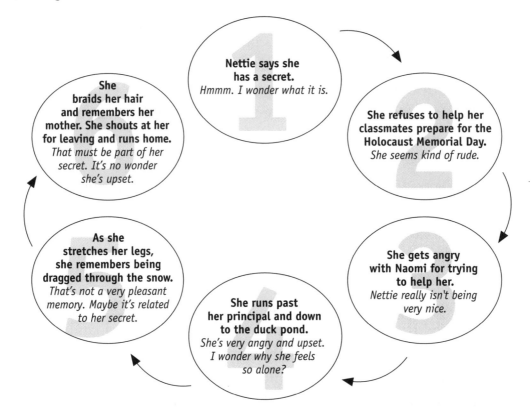

As you continue reading, keep paying attention to Nettie's thoughts, words, and actions. Does she begin to change? At the end of this story, you will finish her character wheel.

Go on reading to see what happens.

Even though I was alone, I closed the door to my room. I opened my closet and knelt down, reaching way into the back. And then I felt the bumpy texture of the leather. I caught at the handle and pulled out the little brown suitcase.

I sat on the floor, carefully balancing the suitcase on my knees. Attached to the thin red cord hanging from the handle were a key and a cardboard tag with my name: *Klagman, Nettie.* Slowly I untied the cord, and the key fell into my palm. Although the lock was red with rust, it popped open quickly. I lifted up the top.

Five things were inside: two photographs glued to the top, a silver ring with a little bell hanging from it, a harmonica, and a scrap of flowered cloth. It was the photographs that I wanted to see. One was of a man and a woman. The woman's hair was blond, with the sunlight shining through it. She was leaning against the man with her cheek on his shoulder, and you couldn't tell if her hair was short or long. He looked straight ahead with dark eyes that were just like mine. Near the corner, in a slanty script, someone had written *Josef and Mira.*

The other photograph was of the same woman, but this time you could see her long blond braid. There was a little girl on her lap, and they were sitting on a garden bench. The little girl's feet already touched the ground, but still the woman held her tightly. I thought of Griselda circling the goslings.

I held my breath and tried to squeeze myself into that picture, into Mira's arms. Then I noticed something I'd never seen before. The scarf on the girl's head was the same flowered material as the scrap in the suitcase.

Mira held the little girl, squinting into the sun and laughing at the same time. Maybe the little girl had said something funny. The same slanty script read *Mira and Nettie, Spring.*

I leaned into the suitcase, smelling it and trying to bring them back, back out of their photographs. And now I could, I really could! I could hear my father playing the harmonica. I heard my mother singing along as she swung me through the air. I could feel the air rushing past and the sky blue and close. "Don't drop me, Momma. Don't drop me."

Then I thought I could hear inside the suitcase the distant clacking of a train. "You're dropping me, Momma!" The train that took them away and left me behind, with the flowered scarf on my head so I wouldn't get cold.

The next day the whole school assembled in the auditorium. The chorus sang lullabies and folk songs, and there were poems and speeches about the importance of remembering. I sat holding the brown suitcase on my lap. Our class was the last to march up onto the stage. David explained the meaning of the yellow Star of David, and Naomi told the story of the Warsaw ghetto. My hands were sweaty on the suitcase handle. They had finished. There was silence and everyone was looking at me.

"Nettie?" Mrs. Levy asked.

I stood up and told my secret.

"I hated my mother and father. My father was Josef Klagman, and he liked to play the harmonica. My mother was Mira Klagman, and I remember her laughing a lot. She had a blond braid just like mine." I opened the suitcase. "These are their pictures—this is what they looked like. They threw me off the train, the train that took them to Auschwitz. They didn't want to leave me. I know that now. I know how much they loved me. Somewhere I know they can hear me.

"Momma, Poppa, Nettie is alive!" ●

Strategy Follow-up

Work on this activity with a partner or a group of classmates. First, on a large piece of paper, draw a character wheel with 11 ovals. Use the information in the Strategy Break to fill in the first 6 ovals. Then use the second part of the story to complete ovals 7–11. Some information is provided below.

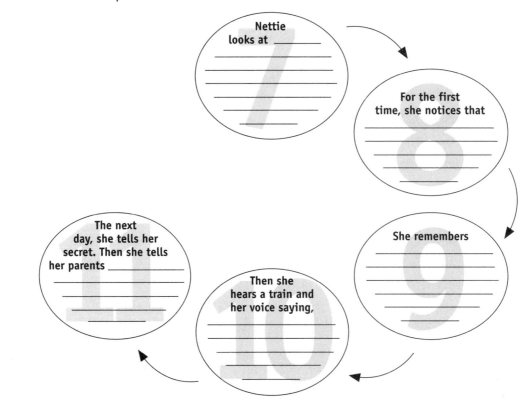

✓ Personal Checklist

Read each question and put a check (✓) in the correct box.

1. How well do you understand what happens in "Five Words"?
    - ☐ 3 (extremely well)
    - ☐ 2 (fairly well)
    - ☐ 1 (not well)

2. In Building Background, how well were you able to list what you know about the Holocaust and use it to make predictions?
    - ☐ 3 (extremely well)
    - ☐ 2 (fairly well)
    - ☐ 1 (not well)

3. How well were you able to complete the word map in the Vocabulary Builder?
    - ☐ 3 (extremely well)
    - ☐ 2 (fairly well)
    - ☐ 1 (not well)

4. How well were you able to help complete the character wheel in the Strategy Follow-up?
    - ☐ 3 (extremely well)
    - ☐ 2 (fairly well)
    - ☐ 1 (not well)

5. How well do you understand Nettie's feelings in this story?
    - ☐ 3 (extremely well)
    - ☐ 2 (fairly well)
    - ☐ 1 (not well)

Vocabulary Check

Look back at the work you did in the Vocabulary Builder. Then answer each question by circling the correct letter.

1. One thing that led to the Holocaust was anti-Semitism. What is anti-Semitism?
    - a. hatred of Jews
    - b. hatred of war
    - c. hatred of trains

2. About how many Jews were killed during the Holocaust?
    - a. one million
    - b. three million
    - c. six million

3. A kibbutz is a community of people who live together. Which context clue from the story could have helped you figure that out?
    - a. "folk dancing"
    - b. "social hall"
    - c. "fast circles"

4. What was considered the most horrible concentration camp during the Holocaust?
    - a. the Warsaw ghetto
    - b. the kibbutz
    - c. Auschwitz

5. In which place in Poland were many Jews forced to live?
    - a. the Warsaw ghetto
    - b. the kibbutz
    - c. Auschwitz

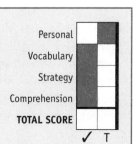

Add the numbers that you just checked to get your Personal Checklist score. Fill in your score here. Then turn to page 209 and transfer your score onto Graph 1.

	Personal	
	Vocabulary	
	Strategy	
	Comprehension	
TOTAL SCORE		
	✓	T

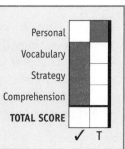

Check your answers with your teacher. Give yourself 1 point for each correct answer, and fill in your Vocabulary score here. Then turn to page 209 and transfer your score onto Graph 1.

	Personal	
	Vocabulary	
	Strategy	
	Comprehension	
TOTAL SCORE		
	✓	T

Strategy Check

Review the character wheel that you helped create in the Strategy Follow-up. Also review the story if necessary. Then answer these questions:

1. How does Nettie feel at the beginning of this story?
   a. She feels angry and alone.
   b. She feels cheerful and helpful.
   c. She feels tired and bored.

2. Which event suggests that Nettie is beginning to change her mind about her parents?
   a. As she braids her hair, she remembers her mother and shouts at her.
   b. She looks inside a little brown suitcase.
   c. She remembers her father playing the harmonica and her mother singing.

3. Why do you think Nettie decides to take part in the Holocaust Memorial Day?
   a. She is tired of the other students giving her a hard time about not participating.
   b. She wants to tell everyone how much she hates her parents for dropping her off the train.
   c. She wants to tell everyone that her parents dropped her off the train to save her life.

4. What conclusion can you draw about Nettie's feelings toward her parents at the end of the story?
   a. She still hates them. She doesn't understand what they did.
   b. She doesn't hate them anymore. She understands what they did.
   c. She's forgotten all about them. She was very young when they died.

5. Why do you think Nettie tells her parents that she is alive?
   a. She wants to thank them for saving her life.
   b. She wants to know if they are still alive too.
   c. She wants them to come and find her.

Comprehension Check

Review the story if necessary. Then answer these questions:

1. Which five words do you think the title of this story refers to?
   a. "Now this is *your* house."
   b. "Momma, Poppa, Nettie is alive!"
   c. "But, Nettie, I didn't mean . . . "

2. Who are Aunt Sara and Uncle Max?
   a. the people who found Nettie and took her in
   b. Nettie's aunt and uncle on her father's side
   c. Nettie's aunt and uncle on her mother's side

3. Why do you think Nettie watches Griselda all the time?
   a. She wishes she had a mother who treated her as Griselda treats her goslings.
   b. Nettie wishes Griselda and her goslings would become her pets.
   c. Griselda reminds Nettie of a beautiful queen in one of her books.

4. What is Nettie's secret?
   a. Uncle Max and Aunt Sara are really her mother and father.
   b. She doesn't want to take part in the Holocaust Memorial Day.
   c. Her parents dropped her from a train when she was a child.

5. Why is Nettie angry about her secret in the beginning of the story?
   a. She doesn't realize that her parents dropped her to save her life.
   b. She doesn't realize that her parents dropped her because they loved her.
   c. Both of the above answers are correct.

Check your answers with your teacher. Give yourself 1 point for each correct answer, and fill in your Strategy score here. Then turn to page 209 and transfer your score onto Graph 1.

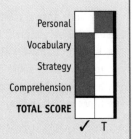

Check your answers with your teacher. Give yourself 1 point for each correct answer, and fill in your Comprehension score here. Then turn to page 209 and transfer your score onto Graph 1.

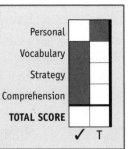

Extending

Choose one or both of these activities:

READ A TRUE STORY OF THE HOLOCAUST

Although it is based on the true stories of many Holocaust survivors, "Five Words" is a work of fiction. There are many true stories written by Holocaust survivors. Use the resources listed on this page to help you find one to read. Share your reactions to the book in an oral or written report.

RESEARCH THE HOLOCAUST

Choose a research partner, and find out more about the Holocaust. Use the sources listed on this page or ones you find yourselves. You might want to begin your research by listing questions that you have about the Holocaust. Then as you do your research, try to find the answers to as many of your questions as possible. Share your findings with the rest of the class.

Resources

Books

Atkinson, Linda. *In Kindling Flame: The Story of Hannah Senesh, 1921–1944.* Morrow, 1985.

Brown, Jean E., Elaine C. Stephens, and Janet E. Rubin. *Images from the Holocaust: A Literature Anthology.* McGraw-Hill, 1996.

Meltzer, Milton. *Rescue: The Story of How Gentiles Saved Jews in the Holocaust.* HarperCollins, 1991.

Rosenberg, Maxine B. *Hiding to Survive: Stories of Jewish Children Rescued from the Holocaust.* Houghton Mifflin, 1998.

Web Sites

http://www.holocaust-history.org/
This is the home page of the Holocaust History Project.

http://www.ushmm.org/
This is the site of the U.S. Holocaust Memorial Museum.

Learning New Words

From Lesson 15
- anti-Semitism

Prefixes

A prefix is a word part that is added to the beginning of a root word. (*Pre-* means "before.") When you add a prefix, you often change the root word's meaning and function. For example, the prefix *re-* means "again," so adding *re-* to the root word *heat* changes the word's meaning to "heat again."

anti-

The prefix *anti-* means "against" or "opposed to." In Lesson 15 you learned that anti-Semitism is hatred of, or prejudice against, Jews. Although *anti-Semitism* is spelled with a hyphen, most words beginning with the prefix *anti-* are not hyphenated.

Match each word with its definition.

antibiotics	liquid that keeps a radiator from freezing
antifreeze	substance that works against swelling
antislavery	substances that fight against infections
anti-inflammatory	against or opposed to slavery

Combining Forms

From Lesson 14
- ambidextrous

A combining form is a word part that is added to another word or combining form to make a new word. For example, *psycho-* is a combining form. If you add it to the word *therapy*, you create the word *psychotherapy*, which means "mental therapy."

ambi-

The combining form *ambi-* means "both." In Lesson 14 you learned that an *ambidextrous* person is someone who can use both hands equally well.

Complete each sentence with one of the words below. Use a dictionary if necessary.

ambivalent   ambiguous   ambiverts

1. When people are both introverts who keep to themselves and extroverts who

    like to socialize, they are _____.

2. Since Jackie didn't care if she went to the movie or not, her feelings were

    _____.

3. Stan's answer was so _____ that we weren't sure what he meant.

Suffixes

A suffix is a word part that is added to the end of a root word. When you add a suffix, you often change the root word's meaning and function. For example, the suffix *-less* means "without," so the root word *pain* changes from a noun to an adjective meaning "without pain."

-ity

The suffix *-ity* turns a word or combining form into a noun that means "the quality, condition, or fact of being ____." In Lesson 14 you learned that an ambidextrous person has good dexterity. The word *dexterity* means "the condition of being skillful with the hands."

Write the word for each definition below.

_____ the quality of being sincere

_____ the condition of being prosperous

_____ the condition of being eligible

_____ the fact of one's ethnic background

-ive

The suffix *-ive* means "having to do with" or "likely to." For example, in "Team Darby" Mark feels protective of his dad when Trent Walker insults him. The word *protective* is an adjective that means "likely to protect."

Write the definition of each word below.

1. active   _____

2. supportive   _____

3. appreciative _____

4. inclusive   _____

VOCABULARY

From Lesson 14
• dexterity

From Lesson 11
• protective

Learning to Disobey

Building Background

There is an old saying that dogs are people's best friends. In no way is this truer than with dogs that are trained to assist people with special needs. Dogs are trained to help people who are blind, deaf, or in wheelchairs. Perhaps most importantly, these dogs are trained to disobey if they think a command would endanger a person. In this article, you will read about "companion animals"—dogs and monkeys—that are trained to help people and make their lives easier.

capuchin monkeys

companion dogs

guide dogs

intelligent disobedience

Vocabulary Builder

1. The words in the margin are from the article you are about to read. Find those words in the statements below. If a statement is true, write a **T** on the line beside it. If a statement is false, write an **F**.

2. If you don't know any of the boldfaced words, guess at their meanings for now. Then, as you read the article, find the words and use context to figure them out. Then go back and write a **T** or an **F** next to those sentences. Double-check your earlier work too, and make any necessary changes.

   _____ a. **Capuchin monkeys** are very smart and can be trained easily.

   _____ b. **Companion dogs** are trained to be people's best friends.

   _____ c. **Guide dogs** are used to take people on guided tours through museums.

   _____ d. Guide dogs will use "**intelligent disobedience**" if it means keeping their companions from harm.

3. Save your work. You will use it again in the Vocabulary Check.

Strategy Builder

Summarizing Nonfiction

- As you know, an **informational article** is nonfiction that gives facts and information about a particular topic. You also know that most nonfiction is organized according to particular patterns. The organizational pattern of "Learning to Disobey" is description. A **description** usually explains how and why something is done or how it works. Most descriptions are organized according to **main ideas** and **supporting details**. These ideas and details help explain or support the topic.

- Sometimes when you read an informational article, you're given a lot of information all at once. To keep the information straight—and to remember it better—you might put the main ideas and details on a concept map. Or you might summarize them. When you **summarize** a section of text, you list or retell the most important ideas in your own words.

- Read the following paragraphs from an article about fishers. Think about how you might summarize the most important ideas.

> Fishers—members of the weasel family—live in North America. They look like house cats, but they have pointed noses. Fishers are small animals, but their speed and strength make them dangerous.
>
> Fishers are meat-eating animals. They attack other creatures for food. Larger, slower animals are easy prey for fishers. Because of their speed, fishers can wear out their enemies and then attack them when they are defenseless.

- How would you summarize the most important ideas in the paragraphs above? Here is how one student did it:

Fishers
- are members of the weasel family
- live in North America
- look like cats with pointed noses
- are small but fast and dangerous
- are meat-eaters that attack and eat other animals

Learning to Disobey

by Margery Facklam

As you read the first part of this article, try to summarize the most important ideas.

Imagine that you are blind. You're standing at a curb, waiting to cross a busy street. You can't see the traffic. Noise surrounds you. Horns honk, motors rumble, people shout, heels click on the sidewalk, and a radio blasts rock music. Your left hand is on the handle of a harness worn by a German shepherd, and you have to trust that dog to take you to the other side of the street. There's a lull in the noise. Has the traffic stopped? You wait for the pull of the harness that tells you to step out, but the dog doesn't move. You give the command "Forward," but the dog disobeys. He stays. Does he see a car that you can't hear?

Guide Dogs

Guide dogs take their companions through shopping malls and supermarkets, and on trains, buses, escalators, and elevators. They are trained to stop at every step up or down, which is why they always stop at curbs. Those kinds of things are easy for a dog to learn. But it must also learn when to disobey a command that would put a blind person in danger. That's not so easy. The trainers at Seeing Eye, Inc. call this "**intelligent disobedience**."

The dogs learn to guide a blind person around fire hydrants, bicycles, and garbage cans. They keep their companions from walking into parked cars and steer them away from children running down the sidewalk. Ordinary dogs pay no attention to low-hanging branches, awnings, or signs. But a guide dog has to understand that its companion can bump his or her head on such obstacles. The dog has to think beyond itself and put itself in another's place.

Guide dogs must be smart, eager, friendly, and patient. Most of them are German shepherds or Labrador retrievers. A puppy selected for this work lives with a family as a pet for a year and a half, learning to get along with people in all kinds of situations. By the time the dog goes back to Seeing Eye for three months of more intensive training, it probably will have gone to church, school, restaurants, and stores with its family. After the dog meets its blind companion, they spend four weeks learning how to work together.

Not every dog graduates from training school, and sometimes a dog and companion aren't right for each other. Poet Desi Vail, who is blind, told me about her second guide dog. "He was the best guide I ever had," she said, "but I couldn't get him to stop chasing squirrels." That dog had to go back to school for further training and eventually became a guide for another blind person. "That's when I got Rainy," she said.

"Do you think Rainy knows you can't see?" I asked her.

"I don't think so," she said. "She just seems to know that I need her help."

 Stop here for the Strategy Break.

Strategy Break

Did you try to summarize the first part of this article? If you did, see if your summary looks anything like this one:

Guide Dogs
- take their companions through places like malls and supermarkets and on trains, buses, elevators, and escalators.
- must learn when to disobey a command that will put a blind person in danger ("intelligent disobedience").
- must learn to guide their companions around things.
- must learn to keep their companions from walking into things.
- must think beyond themselves and put themselves in other people's places.
- must be smart, eager, friendly, and patient.
- are usually German shepherds or Labrador retrievers.
- must live with a family for 1.5 years and go through months of training.
- don't all graduate from training school.
- aren't good companions for everyone.

Go on reading.

Companion Dogs for the Deaf

Companion dogs that live with deaf people learn different tasks, but they, too, have to be smart enough to disobey sometimes. A "hearing ear" dog will nuzzle its owner awake when the alarm clock rings. When it hears a doorbell or a knock on the door, the dog will run back and forth between the door and its companion until the person opens the door. The dog can alert a person to a baby's cry, a ringing telephone, or a smoke alarm. A companion dog for a man who worked outdoors in Texas had to learn the warning sound made by a rattlesnake. When the dog heard a rattler, it did not go toward the snake, but only turned its head in the direction of the sound. That was enough to tell the man he should stay away from a particular clump of grass or pile of rocks.

Many deaf people can drive safely as long as a companion dog sits in the front seat, ready to put a paw on the driver's knee when it hears a siren, honking horn, or screeching tires.

Companion Dogs for People in Wheelchairs

Friendly, easy-going Labrador retrievers are especially good helpers for people in wheelchairs. A group called Canine Companions for Independence gives eight-week-old puppies chosen for this work to families to raise for 14 months. The dogs have to learn 49 commands before they go to advanced training, where they learn to pull a wheelchair, open doors, turn lights on and off, and pick up dropped objects. By the time a dog meets its human partner, it knows 89 commands. Then they both go to a two-week "boot camp," where they learn more about working together.

Now imagine that you are sitting in a wheelchair and can't move your arms or legs. You want to turn on the TV or scratch your nose or get a drink, but you can't. You just have to wait for help. Even a companion dog can't help you, but a monkey can.

Extra Help from Capuchin Monkeys

An organization called Helping Hands trains **capuchin monkeys** to live with people who are paralyzed. The capuchins learn to fetch things that the person points to with the bright light of a laser pointer, which is mounted on the wheelchair and held in the person's mouth. Instead of expecting a monkey to respond to commands such as "Please bring me that magazine on the floor," the person simply points to the magazine. A monkey can turn the pages of a book on a reading stand, or get a wrapped sandwich and unwrap it. The monkey even knows how to get a drink from the refrigerator, open the cap, and insert a straw.

A baby capuchin monkey starts its training by living with a family as a pet for three years. After that, it spends six more months with the Helping Hands teachers. A capuchin monkey learns quickly, especially when it is given a snack reward for doing things right. These monkeys are so bright that they can learn a new task in just one half-hour session, and they don't forget it.

During training and in their owners' houses, the monkeys sleep in large wire-mesh cages. They learn to go to their "rooms" on command and close the door behind them when they have disobeyed and when it's time for a nap or for bed at night. In a corner of the cage, there's a small "toilet," which is a metal pipe with an electric eye in its base. Anything that drops by the electric eye breaks the beam, which triggers a dispenser that sends out a sweet snack reward. One very smart monkey figured out how to get a steady stream of treats after being in his cage only 15 minutes. He dangled an end of his blanket down the pipe. That broke the beam and kept the dispenser open.

A capuchin monkey helper might live its whole life—up to 30 years— with one human companion. In that time, it's likely that the monkey will have to disobey a command now and then in order to help its companion. But these smart little monkeys can handle the job. ●

Strategy Follow-up

On a separate sheet of paper, summarize the rest of this article. Use your own words and the headings Companion Dogs for the Deaf, Companion Dogs for People in Wheelchairs, and Extra Help from Capuchin Monkeys. Be sure to list only the most important ideas, and skip unnecessary details.

✓Personal Checklist

Read each question and put a check (✓) in the correct box.

1. How well do you understand what the title of this article means?
   ☐ 3 (extremely well)
   ☐ 2 (fairly well)
   ☐ 1 (not well)

2. How well do you understand how companion animals make people's lives easier?
   ☐ 3 (extremely well)
   ☐ 2 (fairly well)
   ☐ 1 (not well)

3. In the Vocabulary Builder, how well were you able to decide if each sentence was true or false?
   ☐ 3 (extremely well)
   ☐ 2 (fairly well)
   ☐ 1 (not well)

4. How well were you able summarize the second part of this article?
   ☐ 3 (extremely well)
   ☐ 2 (fairly well)
   ☐ 1 (not well)

5. How well do you understand why capuchin monkeys make good companion animals?
   ☐ 3 (extremely well)
   ☐ 2 (fairly well)
   ☐ 1 (not well)

Vocabulary Check

Look back at the work you did in the Vocabulary Builder. Then answer each question by circling the correct letter.

1. Which phrase describes *intelligent disobedience* as it is used in this article?
   a. learning to disobey a command that will put a person in danger
   b. learning to obey a command that will put a person in danger
   c. learning to obey a command that will help a person out

2. What is one thing that guide dogs might help their companions do?
   a. pay no attention to low-hanging branches
   b. keep from walking into parked cars
   c. put themselves in another person's place

3. According to the article, what kind of dog makes a good companion for a person in a wheelchair?
   a. a Labrador retriever
   b. a French poodle
   c. an Irish setter

4. In what way might a capuchin monkey help its companion?
   a. by waking its companion when the alarm clock rings
   b. by helping its companion drive a car safely
   c. by fetching things that its companion points to with a light

5. According to the article, what is the difference between a guide dog and a companion dog?
   a. There is no difference between a guide dog and a companion dog.
   b. A guide dog helps blind people, and a companion dog helps deaf people.
   c. A companion dog helps blind people, and a guide dog helps people in wheelchairs.

Add the numbers that you just checked to get your Personal Checklist score. Fill in your score here. Then turn to page 209 and transfer your score onto Graph 1.

	Personal	
	Vocabulary	
	Strategy	
	Comprehension	
	TOTAL SCORE	
		✓ T

Check your answers with your teacher. Give yourself 1 point for each correct answer, and fill in your Vocabulary score here. Then turn to page 209 and transfer your score onto Graph 1.

	Personal	
	Vocabulary	
	Strategy	
	Comprehension	
	TOTAL SCORE	
		✓ T

Strategy Check

Review the summaries that you wrote for the second part of this article. Then answer these questions:

1. What is an important idea in the section called Companion Dogs for the Deaf?

    a. Labrador retrievers are especially good helpers for people in wheelchairs.

    b. Companion dogs that live with deaf people have to be smart enough to disobey.

    c. The dogs have to learn 49 commands before they go to advanced training.

2. What is *not* an important idea in Companion Dogs for People in Wheelchairs?

    a. When it hears a doorbell, a dog will run back and forth between the door and its companion.

    b. Friendly Labrador retrievers are especially good helpers for people in wheelchairs.

    c. Capuchin monkeys are so bright that they can learn a new task in a half-hour session.

3. Under which heading would you list the detail that a monkey can turn the pages of a book?

    a. Companion Dogs for the Blind

    b. Companion Dogs for People in Wheelchairs

    c. Extra Help from Capuchin Monkeys

4. Where would you list the detail that a "hearing ear" dog will wake when the alarm clock rings?

    a. Companion Dogs for the Deaf

    b. Companion Dogs for People in Wheelchairs

    c. Extra Help from Capuchin Monkeys

5. Under which heading would you list the detail that by the time a dog meets its human partner, it knows 89 commands?

    a. Companion Dogs for the Blind

    b. Companion Dogs for People in Wheelchairs

    c. Extra Help from Capuchin Monkeys

Comprehension Check

Review the article if necessary. Then answer these questions:

1. Why do you think the author called this article "Learning to Disobey"?

    a. because the article is about animals that learn to disobey commands that could put them in danger

    b. because the article is about animals that learn to disobey commands that could put people in danger

    c. because the article is about people who teach animals commands that could put a person in danger

2. How can a companion dog help a deaf driver?

    a. by barking whenever it hears a siren, a horn, or screeching tires

    b. by putting its paw on the wheel to help the driver steer

    c. by putting its paw on the driver's knee when it hears a siren

3. By the time a companion dog meets its human partner, how many commands does it know?

    a. 14

    b. 49

    c. 89

4. How long does it take a capuchin monkey to learn a new task?

    a. one half-hour

    b. one day

    c. one week

5. What is one thing that a capuchin monkey can do for its companion that a dog cannot do?

    a. It can help its companion drive a car.

    b. It can unwrap a sandwich for its companion.

    c. It can help its companion steer clear of branches.

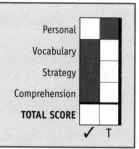

Check your answers with your teacher. Give yourself 1 point for each correct answer, and fill in your Strategy score here. Then turn to page 209 and transfer your score onto Graph 1.

Personal	
Vocabulary	
Strategy	
Comprehension	
TOTAL SCORE	

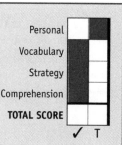

Check your answers with your teacher. Give yourself 1 point for each correct answer, and fill in your Comprehension score here. Then turn to page 209 and transfer your score onto Graph 1.

Personal	
Vocabulary	
Strategy	
Comprehension	
TOTAL SCORE	

Extending

Choose one or more of these activities:

CREATE A BROCHURE OR POSTER

Using the resources listed on this page, find out more about one of the animals discussed in "Learning to Disobey." Then prepare a brochure or a poster that describes your chosen animal. If you'd like, you can use your summaries of this article for additional information.

WRITE AN ANIMAL'S JOURNAL ENTRY

Imagine you are one of the animals described in this article. Using the resources listed on this page or information that you learned from the article, write a journal entry that describes a day in your life. Be sure to mention your companion and what you did to help him or her.

RESEARCH DOG TRAINING

Find out more about training a dog or monkey to assist people with special needs. Choose a task, such as learning to stop for a curb. Then make a list of the steps that would be necessary to train the animal to learn the task. If at all possible, interview a person who trains dogs or monkeys, and have him or her explain or show you the process.

Resources

Books

Emert, Phyllis Raybin. *Guide Dogs*. Working Dogs. Crestwood House, 1985.

Garfield, James B. *Follow My Leader*. Bt Bound, 1999.

Moore, Eva. *Buddy: The First Seeing Eye Dog*. Hello Reader! Cartwheel Books, 1996.

Web Sites

http://guidedogs.com
This is a Web site about guide dogs for the blind.

http://www.caninecompanions.org/
This is the Web site of the Canine Companions for Independence.

http://www.helpinghandsmonkeys.org
On this Web site, learn about the training of capuchin monkeys as helpers for people in wheelchairs.

http://www.lovingpaws.com
This Web site provides information on training dogs to help children with special needs.

Louis Braille and His Dots

Building Background

There is an old saying that necessity is the mother of invention. What do you think it means? Have you ever been faced with a problem that challenged you to find a new or better way of doing something?

Louis Braille, a blind schoolboy in France, had a problem and came up with a solution for it. Louis was frustrated trying to learn to read by tracing large raised letters. In the 1800s, this was the only method of reading for blind people. The necessity of finding a better way led to an important invention. The selection you are about to read is an account of those events.

Braille

cell

dot alphabet

stylus

Vocabulary Builder

1. The words in the margin are all specialized vocabulary words. As you learned in Lesson 4, **specialized vocabulary** words are related to a particular topic. For example, the words *habitats, prey,* and *hibernating* are all related to bears.

2. Read the words in Column 1 below. Draw a line from each word to its definition in Column 2. If you're not sure of a word, find it in the selection and use context to figure it out.

3. Save your work. You will use it again in the Vocabulary Check.

COLUMN 1	COLUMN 2
Braille	box-shaped arrangement of dots
cell	pointed writing tool
dot alphabet	symbols for letters, punctuation, and math
stylus	system of reading for the blind

Strategy Builder

Outlining Main Ideas and Supporting Details

- As you know, **nonfiction** gives facts and details about a particular topic. You also know that most nonfiction is organized according to particular organizational patterns. The pattern of "Louis Braille and His Dots" is description. Most descriptions are organized into **main ideas** and **supporting details**, which explain or support the topic.

- One way to keep track of main ideas and details as you read is to use a concept map. Another way is to summarize them. Still another way is to outline them.

- In the Strategy Builder in Lesson 4, you learned how to arrange main ideas and supporting details about ants on a concept map. Here's how that same information would be arranged in an outline:

Ants

  I. Ants live in communities called colonies.
     A. Some are underground.
     B. Some are in hills.
     C. Some are in trees.
  II. There are three main kinds of ants.
     A. Some are queens.
     B. Some are workers.
     C. Some are in males.
  III. These ants have different jobs.
     A. Queens
       1. They lay eggs.
     B. Workers
       1. Some build and take care of the colony.
       2. Some search for food.
       3. Some take care of the queen's eggs.
     C. Male ants
       1. They mate with queen ants.

Louis Braille and His Dots

by Paulette Bochnig Sharkey

As you begin reading this description, apply the strategies that you just learned. Think about how you might arrange the information on an outline.

Do you know how blind people read? Not with their eyes, but with their fingertips. They can learn to read by touch, thanks to a French boy named Louis Braille.

In the 1820s, Louis attended a special school for blind children in Paris. He and his classmates struggled with the only method of reading available to them: they traced their fingers over heavy paper with big raised letters on it. Reading one letter at a time was slow. And few books were made this way, because it took so long to produce them.

Then Louis heard about "night writing," a code of raised dots and dashes French soldiers used to communicate secretly in the dark. Groups of dots and dashes stood for sounds rather than letters. But a single syllable might have as many as twenty dots—too many to feel at once with one finger—so reading was still slow.

Nevertheless, Louis saw right away that raised dots were easier to read than raised letters. He set to work on his own **dot alphabet**. Three years later, he had found a way to form all the letters, punctuation marks, and mathematical signs using just six dots arranged in a small, box-shaped "**cell**." One fingertip could read all the dots in a cell at once, then quickly move on to the next cell.

Louis's system is now used worldwide, and it's called **Braille** after its inventor. It hasn't changed much in 150 years. A group of raised dots represents each letter of the alphabet. Other sets of dots stand for numbers, punctuation marks, letter combinations like *ch* or *ing*, and common words like *the*.

 Stop here for the Strategy Break.

Strategy Break

If you were to outline the main ideas and supporting details in this selection so far, your outline might look something like this:

Louis Braille and His Dots

I. In the 1820s, Louis Braille and his classmates struggled with the only method of reading available to them.
   A. This method was slow.
   B. There were only a few books made this way.

II. Louis heard about "night writing."
   A. This was a code of raised dots and dashes used to communicate in the dark.
   B. Groups of dots and dashes stood for sounds rather than letters.
   C. A single syllable might have as many as twenty dots, so reading was still slow.

III. Three years later, Louis had developed his own dot alphabet.
   A. Each character, sound, or short word in his system used six dots arranged in a box-shaped cell.
   B. One fingertip could move quickly from cell to cell.
   C. This system—called Braille—is now worldwide and hasn't changed much in 150 years.

As you continue reading, keep paying attention to the main ideas and supporting details. At the end of this selection, you will use some of them to create an outline of your own.

 Go on reading.

Reading and Writing in Braille

Still, Braille creates some problems. For example, Braille books are much thicker than printed ones, because three or four pages of Braille equal one page of type. And Braille must be printed on thick paper, which makes the books even bulkier.

Learning to read Braille takes just as much time and practice as learning to read printed words. After mastering Braille, an average blind reader moves along at one hundred words per minute. That's about half as fast as an average sighted reader.

There are three ways to write in Braille. It can be done by computer, with a program that displays dots on the screen and directs a special printer to make raised dots on paper. Or Braille can be written by hand with a small, pointed tool called a stylus. When the stylus is pressed down on the paper, a dot pops out on the other side. This method is tricky, because the dots must be pressed into the back of the paper, from right to left, the opposite of how they'll appear when the paper is turned over to be read. Some people use a machine that's like a typewriter with only six keys—one for each dot in the Braille cell. Blind children also learn how to use a regular typewriter to write messages to sighted family and friends.

What's Available in Braille?

Just about any kind of reading material someone might want, from newspapers and magazines to cookbooks, schoolbooks, and storybooks. Twin Vision® picture books have Braille pages between the print pages, so sighted people and blind people can read them together. Even music can be translated into Braille. Blind musicians read the notes, memorize them, and play them from memory.

Braille also makes everyday life easier for blind people. One of the first things we all do in the morning is decide what to wear. To help put together matching outfits, blind boys and girls might have Braille labels sewn inside their clothing, identifying the pattern and color. In the kitchen, raised dots on oven dials make cooking easier. Ingredients in jars and cans can also be labeled. You've probably seen Braille number plates in elevators, and Braille signs on public rest-room doors. A Braille watch with raised dots in place of numbers keeps blind people on schedule. And for fun, there are Braille playing cards, Braille versions of popular board games—even Braille baseball cards.

The possibilities are endless. With Louis Braille's wonderful dots, blind people can easily keep "in touch" with the sighted world. ●

BASIC BRAILLE

The Braille alphabet starts with ten combinations of the top four dots in the Braille cell:

a b c d e f g h i j

Adding the lower left dot makes the next ten letters:

k l m n o p q r s t

Adding the lower right dot makes the last five letters (except *w*) and five common words:

u v x y z and for of the with

And removing the lower left dot makes nine common letter pairs, plus the letter *w*:

ch gh sh th wh ed er ou ow w

This method continues until every possible combination of dots is used. Numbers are formed by placing the number sign before the first ten letters:

1 2 3 4 5 6 7 8 9 0

Strategy Follow-up

Work with a group of classmates to complete this activity. First, review the second part of this selection. Then, on a separate sheet of paper, create an outline that begins with **"IV. Reading and Writing in Braille."** Be sure to include only the most important ideas, and skip unnecessary details. If you can, compare your outline with those of other groups. See if your outlines all contain similar information. Revise your group's outline if necessary.

IV. Reading and Writing in Braille

    A.

        1.

        2.

        3.

    B.

        1.

        2.

        3.

    C.

        1.

        2.

    D.

        1.

        2.

        3.

        4.

✓Personal Checklist

Read each question and put a check (✓) in the correct box.

1. How well do you understand how Louis Braille's necessity of finding a better way to read led to an important invention for blind people?
   - ☐ 3 (extremely well)
   - ☐ 2 (fairly well)
   - ☐ 1 (not well)

2. In the Vocabulary Builder, how well were you able to match the specialized vocabulary words and their definitions?
   - ☐ 3 (extremely well)
   - ☐ 2 (fairly well)
   - ☐ 1 (not well)

3. In the Strategy Follow-up, how well were you able to outline the second part of this selection?
   - ☐ 3 (extremely well)
   - ☐ 2 (fairly well)
   - ☐ 1 (not well)

4. How well do you understand how the Braille alphabet works?
   - ☐ 3 (extremely well)
   - ☐ 2 (fairly well)
   - ☐ 1 (not well)

5. How well do you understand why Louis Braille's invention is so important?
   - ☐ 3 (extremely well)
   - ☐ 2 (fairly well)
   - ☐ 1 (not well)

Vocabulary Check

Look back at the work you did in the Vocabulary Builder. Then answer each question by circling the correct letter.

1. In the context of this selection, what is the meaning of *stylus*?
   a. tool used for styling hair
   b. small, pointed writing tool
   c. the needle of a record player

2. In the context of this selection, what is the meaning of *cell*?
   a. box-shaped arrangement of dots
   b. small room in a prison or convent
   c. matter that living things are made of

3. In which sentence is the word *Braille* used correctly?
   a. Harvey learned to read using the Braille system.
   b. Braille developed a system to help blind people read.
   c. *Braille* is used correctly in both of the above sentences.

4. Which phrase best describes Braille?
   a. alphabet of raised dots used to help blind people read and write
   b. alphabet of raised letters that help French soldiers communicate
   c. both of the above

5. What is a dot alphabet?
   a. arrangements of dots that represent shapes, designs, and pictures
   b. arrangements of dots that represent shapes, numbers, and designs
   c. arrangements of dots that represent letters, numbers, and punctuation

Add the numbers that you just checked to get your Personal Checklist score. Fill in your score here. Then turn to page 209 and transfer your score onto Graph 1.

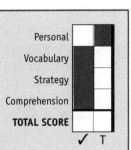

Personal	
Vocabulary	
Strategy	
Comprehension	
TOTAL SCORE	
	✓ T

Check your answers with your teacher. Give yourself 1 point for each correct answer, and fill in your Vocabulary score here. Then turn to page 209 and transfer your score onto Graph 1.

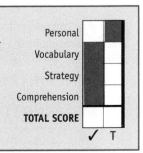

Personal	
Vocabulary	
Strategy	
Comprehension	
TOTAL SCORE	
	✓ T

Strategy Check

Look back at your outline for the second part of this selection. Then answer these questions:

1. Which sentence does *not* state one of this selection's main ideas?

   a. Still, Braille creates some problems.

   b. That's about half as fast as an average sighted reader.

   c. There are three ways to write in Braille.

2. Which sentence *does* state one of this selection's main ideas?

   a. Braille makes everyday life easier for blind people.

   b. An average blind reader can read one hundred words per minute.

   c. Braille can be written by hand with a tool called a stylus.

3. What is one of the problems that Braille creates?

   a. Braille books are much thicker than printed ones.

   b. Even music can be translated into Braille.

   c. There are Braille playing cards and board games.

4. Which is *not* one of the ways to write in Braille?

   a. using a computer with a special printer

   b. using a special typewriter with six keys

   c. using a colored pencil and a sheet of paper

5. What is one of the ways in which Braille makes life easier for blind people?

   a. To put together outfits, blind children might have Braille labels sewn inside their clothing.

   b. When a stylus is pressed down on the paper, a dot pops out on the other side.

   c. Learning to read Braille takes just as much time and practice as learning to read printed words.

Comprehension Check

Review the selection if necessary. Then answer these questions:

1. With which body part or parts do blind people read?

   a. their fingertips

   b. their eyes

   c. their eyes and fingertips

2. Which sentence best describes schooling for the blind in the 1820s?

   a. Reading was quick and easy, and there were lots of books.

   b. Reading was very slow, but there were lots of books.

   c. Reading was very slow, and there were very few books.

3. On which system did Louis Braille base his alphabet?

   a. on a system of big raised letters on heavy paper

   b. on a system of "night writing" used by French soldiers

   c. on a system of big raised letters used by French soldiers

4. How long did it take Louis Braille to develop his dot alphabet?

   a. one year

   b. three years

   c. five years

5. In what way does Braille *not* make life easier for blind people?

   a. Braille helps blind people watch programs on TV.

   b. Raised dots on oven dials make cooking easier.

   c. Braille watches keep blind people on schedule.

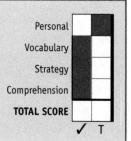

Check your answers with your teacher. Give yourself 1 point for each correct answer, and fill in your Strategy score here. Then turn to page 209 and transfer your score onto Graph 1.

Personal
Vocabulary
Strategy
Comprehension
TOTAL SCORE
✓ T

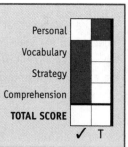

Check your answers with your teacher. Give yourself 1 point for each correct answer, and fill in your Comprehension score here. Then turn to page 209 and transfer your score onto Graph 1.

Personal
Vocabulary
Strategy
Comprehension
TOTAL SCORE
✓ T

Extending

Choose one or more of these activities:

MAKE A POSTER

Learn more about the ways in which Braille makes life easier for blind people. Use the information in the article as well as some of the resources listed on this page. Then make a poster that describes the various uses of Braille. If you can, include pictures on your poster.

RESEARCH LOUIS BRAILLE

Get a copy of Russell Freedman's biography of Louis Braille, which is listed on this page. As you read the book with a partner, take notes on what you are learning. Share this information with the rest of the class.

COMPARE SYSTEMS

Learn about other systems for the blind, such as the New York System of Writing for the Blind. (See the Web sites listed on this page for other systems.) List the main elements of each system and compare and contrast them. How are the systems alike? How are they different? You might use a comparison chart to display your findings.

Resources

Books

Bryant, Jennifer Fisher. *Louis Braille: Inventor.* Great Achievers. Chelsea House, 1994.

Freedman, Russell. *Out of Darkness: The Story of Louis Braille.* Clarion Books, 1999.

Web Sites

http://www.louisbraillecenter.org/learn.htm
Learn more about the Braille system on the Louise Braille Center Web site.

http://www.nyise.org/blind.htm
This is the Web site for the Blindness Resource Center.

http://www.nyise.org/blind/barbier2.htm
This Web page offers information on the history of reading and writing systems for the blind. Clink on "William Bell Wait" to learn about the inventor of the New York System for the Blind.

above

below

danger

day

fell

night

quickly

rose

safety

sick

slowly

well

Building Background

Think about the amusement parks that you have been to or seen. What are your favorite rides? How would you feel if you wanted to ride an enormous roller coaster but you weren't allowed to? In this story, you will read about what happens to Jeff, a boy who must prove that he is strong enough to ride the Mammoth.

Vocabulary Builder

1. The story you are about to read is about a roller coaster. As you know, a roller coaster rolls up and down hills as it goes around a track. The words *up* and *down* are antonyms of each other. **Antonyms** are words with opposite meanings.

2. Study the vocabulary words in the margin. Each word is half of a pair of antonyms. Write the antonym pairs on the clipboards.

3. Then, as you read "The Mammoth," underline any other antonym pairs that you find.

4. Save your work. You will use it again in the Vocabulary Check.

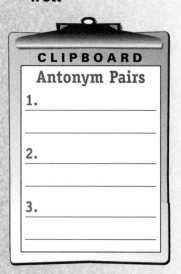

CLIPBOARD
Antonym Pairs
1. _____
   _____
2. _____
   _____
3. _____
   _____

CLIPBOARD
Antonym Pairs
1. _____
   _____
2. _____
   _____
3. _____
   _____

Strategy Builder

Mapping the Elements of a Story

- When you read "A Greenland Rope Trick" in Lesson 5, you learned that one of the main elements of a story is its **plot**, or sequence of events. In most stories, the plot revolves around a **problem** that the main character or characters have and the steps they take to solve it. Another story element is the **setting**—the time and place in which the story happens.

- You also learned how to record the elements of "A Greenland Rope Trick" on a **story map**. If necessary, go back and look at the work you did in that lesson. It will help you complete a story map for "The Mammoth."

The Mammoth

by Michele G. Bonnee

As you begin reading "The Mammoth," keep track of the characters, events, and other important elements. You will use them later to complete a story map.

Jeff Greggins, brown-eyed and bespectacled, didn't notice the storm clouds gathering as he stood enraptured by the mountains of steel rising **above** him. The rails twisted, **rose**, and **fell**, forming a giant silver pathway into the **night**.

"Look at that!" Jeff exclaimed to his father and his cousin Tommy. His eyes widened as a caterpillarlike machine climbed the tallest of the metal peaks. Straight up it went, with bobbing heads and tentacles waving from its body as it inched upward. Suddenly a screech filled the air as the caterpillar edged over the peak and nosed straight down at breakneck speed. The rumbling of metal on metal shook the ground **below** as the machine raced by. Jeff was seeing his very first action-packed roller coaster.

Eagerly, Jeff had waited for the state fair to come. He'd heard other kids talk about The Mammoth, the giant roller coaster that accompanied the fair. Jeff's heart beat rapidly with excitement. The Mammoth was finally here.

"Hey, Dad! Can I go on the roller coaster?" Jeff held his breath for the answer.

Mr. Greggins hesitated, then said, "I don't think you'd better, Jeff. Besides, I'll be pretty busy fixing that Ferris wheel motor. Why don't you boys just wander around for a while until I finish?"

Jeff exhaled **slowly** as the disappointment burned through him. He looked at his cousin. Tommy was disappointed, too. Mr. Greggins patted each boy and started toward the Ferris wheel.

Jeff and Tommy had been helping out at Mr. Greggins' repair shop earlier in the **day** when the telephone rang. A man from the fair's amusement park had called to say that the Ferris wheel motor had blown apart. It was Saturday evening, and Ray Greggins was the only repairman available. The boys were delighted when Mr. Greggins asked them to go with him.

But now, what difference does it make? Jeff thought. *We might as well have stayed at home.* Jeff knew the real reason his dad wouldn't let him ride the roller coaster. Jeff had been **sick** for a good portion of his life. When he was born, his heart didn't work the way it should. He'd had several operations, the last one a year ago. The doctor had assured Jeff and his parents that Jeff's heart was as good as new and that there would be no further need for operations. "You can do anything other kids do," the doctor had said.

Jeff didn't think his dad believed the doctor. *Other* kids got to ride roller coasters.

Embarrassed, Jeff said, "I'm sorry, Tommy. It's my fault we can't go. Dad thinks I'll never be **well** enough."

"That's OK, Jeff." Tommy's eyes sparkled with renewed hope. "Maybe we can go on some other rides. I'll go ask Uncle Ray if we can. Wait here." Tommy ran to find his uncle.

Jeff propped against the ticket booth, taking in the scene around him. He felt like a spectator on a circus movie set.

Costumed clowns strolled merrily by, carrying rainbows of balloons. Striped-shirted barkers called to passersby, offering them chances to win the assortment of stuffed animals arranged neatly behind them. Popcorn, hot dog, and soda pop stands lined the park, tantalizing the hungry patrons. Children stood nearby, grasping snow cones and pink cotton candy with sticky fingers.

Chatter and laughter filled the air. Jeff sauntered below the bright-colored lights outlining the tracks of the mountainous roller coaster. One thought repeated in his head: *I wish I could ride The Mammoth just one time.*

A deep rumbling aroused Jeff from his thoughts. Expecting the coaster car to round the bend in front of him, Jeff jumped back when a flash of light ripped through the dark sky. The sky lit up as if illuminated by a giant flashbulb. An ear-splitting clap of thunder boomed. The park lights dimmed, then brightened in response. But the lights along the roller coaster tracks went out completely.

 Stop here for the Strategy Break.

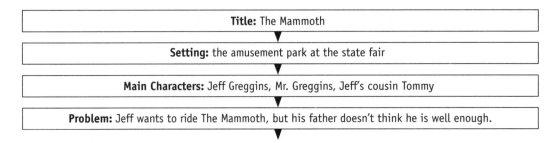

Strategy Break

If you were to create a story map for "The Mammoth" so far, it might look like this:

Title: The Mammoth

▼

Setting: the amusement park at the state fair

▼

Main Characters: Jeff Greggins, Mr. Greggins, Jeff's cousin Tommy

▼

Problem: Jeff wants to ride The Mammoth, but his father doesn't think he is well enough.

▼

Events:
1. When Jeff, his cousin Tommy, and his dad arrive at the state fair, Jeff asks his dad if he can ride The Mammoth.
2. Jeff's dad tells the boys to wander around until he is finished with the Ferris wheel.
3. Tommy goes to ask his uncle if they can go on some of the other rides.
4. As Jeff stands watching the Mammoth, the lights along its track go out.

▼

To be continued . . .

As you continue reading, keep paying attention to the events in this story. You will use them to complete the story map in the Strategy Follow-up.

 Go on reading to see what happens.

Screams broke the silence brought on by the thunder. These were not the screams of fun-seekers, but cries of fear. Jeff glimpsed a reflection of metal on the lenses of his glasses. He spotted an electric wire swinging danger-ously near the stalled coaster car, which was trapped high above him in one of the metal valleys. Jeff glanced toward the control center. No one was around.

Jeff knew something had to be done immediately. His father had told him that electricity was to be respected. Unleashed, it could hurt people. The broken cable, whipping in the wind like a dragon spitting fiery threats, was blowing closer to the car.

Jeff had to act **quickly**. He ran to the central controls. He found the outlet to the coaster, but the runaway cable's source of electricity was not there. Following the wire closely with his eyes, Jeff began to run along its length, looking for its power supply.

Moving under the cable, he noticed how snakelike it seemed as it came close to striking the frightened occupants of the car. Finally, Jeff spotted the power source. A small electrical box, suspended on a pole next to the tracks, was where the cable originated. The box was fifty feet above Jeff's head. He would have to climb the tracks.

While recuperating from his operations, Jeff had daydreamed of many adventures. He had climbed mountains and trees, been a hero to soldiers, captain of the soccer team, even a space shuttle pilot. But this time the adventure was real.

Jeff began to climb. Below, people gathered. Horrified, they yelled for him to come down. But Jeff kept climbing. Carefully he stepped from one metal plank to the next. Reaching the box, he opened it, flipped the power switch off, and turned to see the cable crackle its threat for the last time. Falling to the ground, it brushed the car—but the **danger** had passed. The fiery dragon, the electrical snake, had died.

Sirens sounded as the fire and rescue trucks arrived. Soon firemen were craning their ladders to the stranded car. One by one, each victim was brought to **safety**.

Jeff climbed slowly and carefully down from the tracks. Waiting below, his anxious father and cousin ran toward him. They had come to look for Jeff when the lightning struck, but hadn't expected to find him atop the roller coaster tracks!

Mr. Greggins pulled his son close and hugged him hard. Breathless with excitement, Jeff recounted the events to the eager listeners. Then Mr. Greggins said, "I'm so glad you're all right. Don't you know you could have been hurt? The climb, too much excitement, your heart . . ."

"Dad, I'm OK," Jeff interrupted. "I did just what you taught me to do in an electrical emergency. I stopped it from going crazy." He paused. "Just like the doctor fixed my heart when it was acting crazy. Now everything is OK here, too," he said, pointing to his chest.

The man who owned the park ran to Jeff. "I saw what you did. You really knew what you were doing. Thank you! You saved a lot of people from being hurt. You can come and ride all the rides any time you want." The man handed Jeff a free pass.

Mr. Greggins smiled. "I guess it is time I let you do more. I suppose you want to start with riding The Mammoth!" he joked.

Jeff looked skeptical. "I think I've had enough adventure for one night. Maybe I'll just settle for a car ride home." Everyone laughed as the three-some headed for the parking lot. ●

Strategy Follow-up

Now complete the story map for "The Mammoth." Start the map with Event 5. Parts of the events have been filled in for you.

Problem: Jeff wants to ride The Mammoth, but his father doesn't think he is well enough.

▼

Event 5: Jeff sees

▼

Event 6: He spots the power source, but

▼

Event 7: He climbs

▼

Event 8: When his father starts to remind Jeff about his heart,

▼

Solution:

✓Personal Checklist

Read each question and put a check (✓) in the correct box.

1. How well were you able use your knowledge of amusement parks and roller coasters to understand what happens in this story?
    - ☐ 3 (extremely well)
    - ☐ 2 (fairly well)
    - ☐ 1 (not well))

2. How well were you able to match the antonym pairs in the Vocabulary Builder?
    - ☐ 3 (extremely well)
    - ☐ 2 (fairly well)
    - ☐ 1 (not well)

3. How well were you able to complete the story map in the Strategy Follow-up?
    - ☐ 3 (extremely well)
    - ☐ 2 (fairly well)
    - ☐ 1 (not well)

4. How well do you understand why Jeff wants to ride The Mammoth so badly in the beginning of this story?
    - ☐ 3 (extremely well)
    - ☐ 2 (fairly well)
    - ☐ 1 (not well))

5. How well do you understand why Mr. Greggins says Jeff can ride The Mammoth at the end of the story?
    - ☐ 3 (extremely well)
    - ☐ 2 (fairly well)
    - ☐ 1 (not well)

Vocabulary Check

Look back at the work you did in the Vocabulary Builder. Then answer each question by circling the correct letter.

1. Which antonym pair can be used to describe a person's health?
    - a. sick/well
    - b. day/night
    - c. quickly/slowly

2. Which vocabulary word is the antonym of *danger*?
    - a. night
    - b. quickly
    - c. safety

3. The antonym of *slowly* is *quickly*. Which other word from the story is also an antonym of *slowly*?
    - a. straight
    - b. rapidly
    - c. upward

4. Which antonym pair could describe the motion of The Mammoth as it goes around the track?
    - a. quickly/slowly
    - b. rose/fell
    - c. both of the above

5. While looking for the power source, Jeff discovers that the electrical box is 50 feet above his head. What is the antonym of *above*?
    - a. below
    - b. night
    - c. danger

Add the numbers that you just checked to get your Personal Checklist score. Fill in your score here. Then turn to page 209 and transfer your score onto Graph 1.

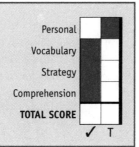

Check your answers with your teacher. Give yourself 1 point for each correct answer, and fill in your Vocabulary score here. Then turn to page 209 and transfer your score onto Graph 1.

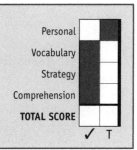

Strategy Check

Review the story map that you completed in the Strategy Follow-up. Then answer these questions:

1. What does Jeff see after the lights go out along the roller coaster track?

    a. the screams of people in the roller coaster cars

    b. an electric wire swinging near a stalled roller coaster car

    c. a piece of metal swinging dangerously near his glasses

2. Why does Jeff start climbing the tracks of The Mammoth?

    a. He wants to jump into The Mammoth and go for a ride.

    b. He wants to get back at his father for not letting him ride.

    c. He wants to get to the power source to turn off the power.

3. During which event does Mr. Greggins tell Jeff that he can ride The Mammoth?

    a. Event 6

    b. Event 7

    c. the solution

4. What is the solution to Jeff's problem?

    a. Jeff gets a free pass, and Mr. Greggins says he can ride The Mammoth.

    b. Jeff finally gets to ride on The Mammoth with his dad and his cousin.

    c. Jeff's dad gets angry with Jeff for risking his health and takes him home.

5. Why is the solution ironic?

    a. Now that Jeff has a pass and permission to ride The Mammoth, he doesn't want to.

    b. Now that Jeff has a pass and permission to ride The Mammoth, he gets sick.

    c. Now that Jeff has a pass and permission to ride The Mammoth, it doesn't run.

Comprehension Check

Review the story if necessary. Then answer these questions:

1. Why were Jeff, his dad, and his cousin at the state fair?

    a. They were there to have a good time.

    b. They were there to test every ride.

    c. They were there to repair the Ferris wheel.

2. In the beginning of the story, why doesn't Mr. Greggins want Jeff to ride The Mammoth?

    a. He doesn't think Jeff is well enough.

    b. He thinks that Jeff will be too afraid.

    c. He wants to punish Jeff and Tommy.

3. How does Jeff know what to do about the roller coaster?

    a. His father had taught him about electrical emergencies.

    b. The person at the control center tells him what to do.

    c. He doesn't know—he fixes the problem by accident.

4. What causes Mr. Greggins to change his mind about letting Jeff go on the roller coaster?

    a. When the park owner gives Jeff a pass, Mr. Greggins realizes he won't have to pay.

    b. Jeff tells Mr. Greggins that the doctor fixed his heart, just as Jeff fixed the roller coaster.

    c. Both of the above answers are correct.

5. Why does Jeff decide not to ride The Mammoth after all?

    a. He says he's had enough adventure for one night.

    b. His heart is bothering him after all that excitement.

    c. Both of the above answers are correct.

Check your answers with your teacher. Give yourself 1 point for each correct answer, and fill in your Strategy score here. Then turn to page 209 and transfer your score onto Graph 1.

Personal
Vocabulary
Strategy
Comprehension
TOTAL SCORE
✓ T

Check your answers with your teacher. Give yourself 1 point for each correct answer, and fill in your Comprehension score here. Then turn to page 209 and transfer your score onto Graph 1.

Personal
Vocabulary
Strategy
Comprehension
TOTAL SCORE
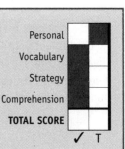
✓ T

Extending

Choose one or more of these activities:

WRITE A NEW CHAPTER

Imagine that "The Mammoth" is Chapter Two in a book about Jeff Greggins. With a partner or a small group of classmates, brainstorm what Jeff's life was like both before and after this chapter. Then choose one chapter to write about. Chapter One could describe Jeff's life before the surgery that makes him well. Chapter Three could describe Jeff's life after the surgery. (If you'd like, you can write about Jeff's next visit to an amusement park.) Be sure to use a story map as you plan your chapter.

ILLUSTRATE "THE MAMMOTH"

The author of this story uses many vivid details to describe The Mammoth. Find some of those details and use them to illustrate a few scenes from this story. The phrases below will help you get started.

- caterpillarlike machine . . . with bobbing heads and tentacles waving from its body as it inched upward

- the rails twisted, rose and fell, forming a giant silver pathway into the night

- the fiery dragon, the electrical snake

DESIGN YOUR OWN ROLLER COASTER

If you could design the roller coaster of your dreams—or nightmares—what would it look like? What would you name it, and why? Sketch your roller coaster, or build it out of toothpicks or some other material. Then explain it to your class. Use some of the resources on this page if you need help getting started.

Resources

Books

Alter, Judy. *Amusement Parks: Roller Coasters, Ferris Wheels, and Cotton Candy.* First Books. Franklin Watts, 1997.

Duffey, Betsy. *Coaster.* Viking Children's Books, 1994.

Roberts, Willo Davis. *Scared Stiff.* Aladdin, 2001.

Web Sites

http://www.learner.org/exhibits/parkphysics/coaster/
This interactive Web site helps you design your own roller coaster.

http://www.rcdb.com
This Web site has a roller coaster database that allows you to search for information and pictures related to roller coasters around the world.

Mayday!

Building Background

People around the world use the word *Mayday* to let others know that they are in trouble. Mayday is an international radio call that comes from a French word meaning "help me." Think about stories that you have read or seen on TV in which someone calls for help using Mayday. How did those stories turn out?

In the story you are about to read, what do you predict will cause the characters to call Mayday? How do you predict the story will turn out? Why?

animated

astonishment

inexplicable

Mayday

monologue

turbulence

Vocabulary Builder

1. The words in the margin are all from "Mayday!" Knowing these words will help you understand the story better.

2. Read each boldfaced vocabulary word below and think about what it means. (Use a dictionary if you need help.) Then read the three words that follow it. Cross out the one word that is not related to the others. The first item has been done for you.

animated	lively	drawn	excited
astonishment	boredom	amazement	shock
inexplicable	unexplainable	mysterious	well-known
Mayday	first of May	danger sign	distress call
monologue	solo speech	chorus	single speaker
turbulence	disturbance	uproar	calm

3. Save your work. You will use it again in the Vocabulary Check.

Strategy Builder

Making Predictions While Reading a Story

- When you read a story, you often make predictions. As you learned in Lesson 1, a **prediction** is a kind of guess that you make based on information or clues that the author provides. Those clues are called **context** clues. They "set the scene" and help you understand what's happening. They also help you predict what might happen next.

- As you read "Mayday!" you will pause twice to make predictions. At Strategy Break #1, you will write down your predictions. You also will write which context clues helped you make your predictions.

- At Strategy Break #2, you will check your earlier predictions. Then you will make more predictions, and you will tell which clues helped you make them.

- After you finish reading the story, you will see if any of your predictions matched what happened in the story.

Mayday!

by Redvers Brandling

See if you can use the clues that the author provides to help you make predictions while you read.

Captain Ian Sercombe was frightened. He rested a broad forefinger on the control column of the Boeing 747 and eased back in his seat. Glancing out of the cabin windows at the sixty meters of his giant machine's wingspan, he tried to calm himself with thoughts of its size and detail . . . as high as a six-story building, over 200 kilometers of wiring, 4 million parts, space for more than 400 passengers . . .

"Decent night, Skip."

First Officer Les Bright's voice cut in on Ian's thoughts. The two men had completed the pre-takeoff check and were sitting on the flight deck. Outside, a huge moon hung in the hot tropical night sky, which pressed down on Singapore's Changi Airport.

Les Bright was talking to the control tower when Cabin Service Director Edwina Reeves came into the flight deck area.

"Two hundred and sixty passengers and thirteen cabin crew are safely on board, Captain. Cabin secure."

"Thanks, Edwina," replied Ian. "We should be off very soon."

Minutes later the huge aircraft began to roll away from its stand at the airport. The time was 8:04 P.M., and the journey to Perth, Australia, had begun.

Within an hour all was routine on the flight deck. The jumbo was cruising at Flight Level 370, about seven miles above sea level. Speed was 510 knots, the course was 160° magnetic, and the plane, under the automatic pilot, headed south over Indonesia.

"Weather ahead looks good," commented First Officer Bright, nodding at the weather radar screen, which promised three hundred miles of smooth flying ahead.

He had been studying the weather radar with unusual intensity—just as he had all the other complex instruments in the cabin. But the fear wouldn't go away. It wasn't nervousness . . . or apprehension . . . Ian Sercombe was frightened. He could only ever remember feeling like this once before, and that had been the dreadful day of the accident. . . .

Ian and his lifelong friend Mike Payne had been crewing together on a flight back from New York. Leaving the airport in Ian's car, they were accelerating on the M25 when a tire burst. In the crash that followed, Ian had been unhurt, but Mike was killed instantly. Just before the tire went, Ian had felt this unreasoning fear. Afterward he could never quite rid himself of guilt for Mike's death. He'd been blameless perhaps—he'd checked the tires just a couple of days previously—but how could Mike know that? Once again he thought of Mike's bluff, smiling Irish face, grinning as always and how he clapped those gloved hands together. That had always been a joke between them—the only pilot who never flew without wearing fine kid gloves.

Ian's thoughts were brought back to the present as First Officer Bright made a routine position report.

"Jakarta Control, Moonlight Seven over Halim at 20:44."

Then it started.

"Unusual activity on weather radar, Captain."

"I see it, Les."

"Just come up—doesn't look good."

"Could be some **turbulence** in that. Switch on the 'Fasten Seat Belts' sign."

 Stop here for Strategy Break #1.

Strategy Break #1

1. What do you predict will happen next? _____

_____

2. Why do you think so? _____

_____

3. What clues from the story helped you make your prediction(s)? _____

_____

 Go on reading to see what happens.

The two pilots tightened their own seat belts. Behind them in the crowded cabins, passengers grumbled as they had to interrupt their evening meal to fasten their seat belts. Smiling stewardesses assured them there was no problem.

"Engine failure—Four!" The flight engineer's terse voice cut the flight deck silence.

"Fire action Four," responded Ian simultaneously.

Together Les Bright and Engineer Officer Mary Chalmers shut off the fuel lever to Four and pulled the fire handle. There was no fire in the engine, and Ian felt an easing of his tension.

No pilot likes an engine failure, but the giant jumbo could manage well enough on the three that were left.

"Engine failure Two."

Mary Chalmers's voice was more urgent this time, but as she and Les Bright moved to another emergency procedure, she suddenly gasped breathlessly.

"One's gone . . . and Three!"

Seven miles high with 273 people on board, the Boeing was now without power. Ian knew that the huge plane could only glide—and downward.

"**Mayday**, Mayday, Mayday!" First Officer Bright's voice barked into the emergency radio frequency. "Moonlight Seven calling. Complete failure on all engines. Now descending through Flight Level 360."

Ian's hands and mind were now working with automatic speed. He again checked the fuel and electrical systems. Emergency restarting procedures failed to have any effect. Quickly he calculated their terrible position. The plane was dropping at about two hundred feet per minute . . . which meant that in twenty-three minute's time . . .

"You two," said Ian quietly to the first officer and flight engineer. "I'm going to need all the help I can get later on, but there could be problems back there with the passengers now—especially as we're obviously going down. Go back—help out—and get back here as soon as you can."

Bright and Chalmers climbed out of their seats, slamming the door to the flight deck behind them as they went to try to reassure the terrified passengers.

Ian was now alone on the flight deck.

"Problems," he muttered aloud. "Crash landing in the sea, so keep the wheels up; lights are going to fail because there's no generated power from the engines; standby power from the batteries won't last long. . . ."

Stop here for Strategy Break #2.

Strategy Break #2

1. Do your earlier predictions match what happened? _____ Why or why not? _____
_____

2. What do you predict will happen next? _____
_____

3. Why do you think so? _____
_____

4. What clues from the story helped you make your prediction(s)? _____
_____
_____

 Go on reading to see what happens.

The closing of the flight deck door interrupted Ian's **monologue**.

"All right back there?" he asked as the First Officer climbed back into his seat. He was just able to make out his fellow pilot's quick nod in the rapidly dimming light on the flight deck.

"It's too risky to try and get over those mountains now," said Ian. "What do you think?"

"Go for the sea," was the reply, in a strangely muffled tone.

Ian's arms were aching from holding the lurching and buffeting aircraft, but he was surprised when the First Officer leaned over and laid a hand on his shoulder. It seemed to have both a calming and a strengthening effect.

"I'll take her for a while."

The giant plane continued to drop. At 14,000 feet the emergency oxygen masks had dropped from the roof for passengers' use. Now the rapidly dropping height was down to 13,000 feet.

"I'll save myself for the landing," muttered Ian, watching his copilot in admiration. In the dim light the First Officer was a relaxed figure, almost caressing the jerking control column. His touch seemed to have calmed the aircraft, too. Its descent seemed smoother, almost gentle even.

13,000. 12,000. 11,000. "Ian."

The captain was startled by the unexpected use of his Christian name by the First Officer.

"Volcanic dust and jet engines don't mix. I think we should make another relight attempt on the engines now."

Still feeling calm, even relaxed considering the terrible situation they were in, Ian began the engine restarting drill yet again.

"Switch on igniters . . . open fuel valves . . ."

As suddenly as it had failed, Engine Four sprang back into life.

"We've got a chance!" cried Ian.

"Go for the rest," was the quiet reply.

Expertly, Ian's hands repeated the procedure. There was a lengthy pause then . . . bingo! Number Three fired . . . then One . . . and then Two.

"We'll make it after all," sighed Ian, once again taking a firm grip of the controls. "Les—get on to Jakarta Control and tell them what's happening ... "

To his **astonishment**, when Ian looked to his right, only the gently swaying control column came into view. It was then that the captain heard the crash of the ax breaking through the door to the flight deck.

Engineer Chalmers was the first one through the shattered door.

"Fantastic, Skipper, fantastic—how did you do it?"

"Incredible!" This was Les Bright's voice.

"The flight deck door jammed, and we've been stuck out there for five minutes wondering how on earth you were getting on—and now this! You're a marvel Skipper." Ian glanced up at the **animated** face of his First Officer in the brightening light of the flight deck.

"But . . ."

The rest of the words died on his lips. A feeling of **inexplicable** calm swept over him. He remembered the confident, sure figure who had so recently sat in the copilot's seat. He now remembered, too, that just before the lights had reached their dimmest, he had noticed that the hands holding the controls were wearing a pair of fine kid gloves.

"Get on to Jakarta," Ian said quietly. "Tell them we're coming in." ●

Strategy Follow-up

Go back and look at the predictions that you wrote in this lesson. Do any of them match what actually happened in this story?_____ Why or why not?

_____

✓Personal Checklist

Read each question and put a check (✓) in the correct box.

1. How well do you understand what happens in this story?
   - ☐ 3 (extremely well)
   - ☐ 2 (fairly well)
   - ☐ 1 (not well)

2. How well were you able to use the information in Building Background to understand why this story is called "Mayday!"?
   - ☐ 3 (extremely well)
   - ☐ 2 (fairly well)
   - ☐ 1 (not well)

3. In the Vocabulary Builder, how well were you able to cross out the words that did not belong?
   - ☐ 3 (extremely well)
   - ☐ 2 (fairly well)
   - ☐ 1 (not well)

4. How well were you able to use context clues to predict what would happen next in this story?
   - ☐ 3 (extremely well)
   - ☐ 2 (fairly well)
   - ☐ 1 (not well)

5. How well do you understand who or what helps Ian Sercombe keep the plane from crashing?
   - ☐ 3 (extremely well)
   - ☐ 2 (fairly well)
   - ☐ 1 (not well)

Vocabulary Check

Look back at the work you did in the Vocabulary Builder. Then answer each question by circling the correct letter.

1. What are the passengers usually told to do when a plane hits some turbulence?
   a. fasten their seatbelts
   b. put out their cigarettes
   c. stop talking to each other

2. Which phrase best describes what the word *Mayday* means?
   a. Suppertime!
   b. Help me!
   c. Hey there!

3. How many people are speaking during a monologue?
   a. one
   b. two
   c. five

4. What element of this story could be described as inexplicable?
   a. The plane is leaving Singapore and is on its way to Perth, Australia.
   b. Two hundred sixty passengers and thirteen cabin crew are on board.
   c. The door is jammed shut, but there is a person in the cabin with Ian.

5. In the context of this story, which word best defines the word *animated*?
   a. lively
   b. excited
   c. drawn

Add the numbers that you just checked to get your Personal Checklist score. Fill in your score here. Then turn to page 209 and transfer your score onto Graph 1.

Personal	
Vocabulary	
Strategy	
Comprehension	
TOTAL SCORE	✓ T

Check your answers with your teacher. Give yourself 1 point for each correct answer, and fill in your Vocabulary score here. Then turn to page 209 and transfer your score onto Graph 1.

Personal	
Vocabulary	
Strategy	
Comprehension	
TOTAL SCORE	✓ T

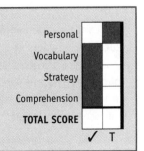

Strategy Check

Look back at what you wrote at each Strategy Break. Then answer these questions:

1. If you had predicted that the plane would have trouble, which clue below would have best supported your prediction?
   a. "Weather ahead looks good."
   b. "Two hundred and sixty passengers . . . safely on board, Captain."
   c. "Could be some turbulence. . . . Switch on the 'Fasten Seat Belts' sign."

2. At Strategy Break #2, which prediction would have best fit the story?
   a. The batteries will keep the plane running.
   b. The plane will crash-land in the sea.
   c. The engines will begin running again.

3. If you had predicted that the plane would crash, which clue would have best supported your prediction?
   a. Smiling stewardesses assured them there was no problem.
   b. There was no fire in the engine, and Ian felt an easing of his tension.
   c. "Problems. Crash landing in the sea, . . . "

4. What was the best clue to the identity of the copilot who saved the plane from crashing?
   a. The First Officer was a relaxed figure.
   b. The captain was startled by the unexpected use of his Christian name.
   c. The hands holding the controls were wearing a pair of fine kid gloves.

5. Which clue explains why the plane didn't crash?
   a. "Make another relight attempt on the engines."
   b. It was then that the captain heard the ax breaking though the door to the flight deck.
   c. "Get on to Jakarta," Ian said quietly. "Tell them we're coming in."

Comprehension Check

Review the story if necessary. Then answer these questions:

1. Why do you think the author called this story "Mayday!"?
   a. It's a clue that nothing exciting will happen.
   b. It's a clue that something life-threatening will happen.
   c. It's a clue that something will happen on the first of May.

2. What earlier event in Ian's life had also caused him to feel frightened?
   a. He felt frightened just before he was in an earlier plane crash.
   b. He felt frightened just before he saw turbulence on the weather screen.
   c. He felt frightened just before he was in a car crash that killed his friend.

3. What causes the engines to fail on the Boeing 747?
   a. Ian doesn't know.
   b. A volcano erupts, and the dust clogs the engines.
   c. Turbulence knocks out all of the engines.

4. Why does Ian turn over the plane's controls to the First Officer?
   a. Ian says he'll save himself for the landing.
   b. The First Officer grabs the controls from him.
   c. Ian wants to go back and check on the passengers.

5. Why do you think a feeling of calm sweeps over Ian at the end of the story?
   a. He is proud that he saved the plane from crashing.
   b. He is happy that his crew thinks he's a marvel.
   c. He feels he was helped by his friend Mike Payne.

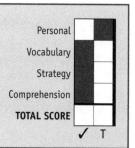

Check your answers with your teacher. Give yourself 1 point for each correct answer, and fill in your Strategy score here. Then turn to page 209 and transfer your score onto Graph 1.

Personal
Vocabulary
Strategy
Comprehension
TOTAL SCORE
✓ T

Check your answers with your teacher. Give yourself 1 point for each correct answer, and fill in your Comprehension score here. Then turn to page 209 and transfer your score onto Graph 1.

Personal
Vocabulary
Strategy
Comprehension
TOTAL SCORE
✓ T

Extending

Choose one or more of these activities:

WRITE A JOURNAL ENTRY

Imagine you are Captain Ian Sercombe, and you've just gotten to your hotel room in Jakarta. Write a journal entry that describes what happened on the plane. Be sure to include your thoughts and feelings at various times during the flight.

TELL STORIES AROUND A "CAMPFIRE"

Read other stories with surprise endings, and then tell them to a group of classmates. (See the resources listed on this page, and check the Internet.) With permission, set up a corner of the room to look like a campfire. Then turn off the lights and share your stories. Take a vote on which story or stories everyone likes best.

RESEARCH REAL AIR DISASTERS

Find out more about major air disasters by using the Internet or other sources. Find out information such as when and where each disaster occurred, what caused it, what type of plane it was, how many passengers were on board, and how many of them survived. You might want to present your findings on a comparison chart.

Resources

Books

Cooney, Caroline B. *Flight #116 Is Down!* Scholastic, 1993.

Goodman, Burton. *Surprise.* Glencoe/McGraw-Hill, 1990.

Strasser, Todd. *Gater Prey.* Against the Odds. Minstrel Books, 1999.

Web Site

http://www.planecrashinfo.com/
This Web site provides information on major civilian air disasters from the early 1900s to the present.

A Trickle in the Desert

Building Background

What would life be like if you lived where almost no rain fell? Can you imagine living without fresh water? By yourself or with a partner, list some of the problems that you would face. How might you try to solve them?

In "A Trickle in the Desert" you will read about a village in Chile where rain rarely falls. You also will read about the amazing but simple way in which scientists are helping people solve this problem.

camanchacas

evaporates

harsh

luxury

skeptical

Vocabulary Builder

1. The words in the margin are from "A Trickle in the Desert." Read the words, and then use them to complete the paragraph below. Use context clues to help you if you don't know what a word means. If context clues don't help, use a dictionary.

2. Save your work. You will use it again in the Vocabulary Check.

Life without fresh water can be tough and _____.

It is a _____ just to take a bath. Fogs, called

_____ in Chile, might be a source of fresh water.

But too often, the fogs _____ before they reach the

village. Scientists thought that they had an answer to the water problem.

But the villagers were _____. They didn't think it

would work.

Strategy Builder

Identifying Problems and Solutions in Nonfiction

- As you know, every piece of nonfiction has an organizational pattern. The most common patterns are description, cause-effect, sequence, and compare-contrast. Another organizational pattern, however, is **problem-solution**. When a piece of writing follows this pattern, the problem is first described, and then the solution or solutions are presented. To see this pattern more clearly, you can put the information on a **problem-solution frame**.

- As you just read in Building Background and the Vocabulary Builder, the problem described in "A Trickle in the Desert" is a lack of fresh water. Now read the article to find out why it was a problem and what solutions people tried to solve it.

A Trickle in the Desert

by Laila S. Khalil

Life in Chungungo was **harsh**. The village sits on the coast of Chile, between the Pacific Ocean and El Tofo Mountain. But the people had almost no fresh water.

There is no river or lake nearby. Rain rarely falls. So there were no gardens. There were no trees. Many people left their homes and moved south, where they could have water and electricity. But 350 people stayed in Chungungo.

These villagers lived by fishing in the ocean. They painted their homes bright orange or green or blue. And they hired trucks to haul water to the village from a well twenty-five miles away.

Trucking their water was so expensive that each villager could afford to use only four gallons of water a day. (On average, most people in the United States and Canada use about ninety gallons a day.) In Chungungo, bathing in fresh water was a **luxury**.

Life in Chungungo might have been better. Almost constantly, clouds flow in from the Pacific Ocean toward El Tofo Mountain. But these clouds pass over the coast, dropping very little rain.

When a cloud plows into El Tofo and the other mountains that line the coast, the cloud is called a fog simply because it is touching the earth. Each of these fogs, called a *camanchaca*, rolls over the mountains. Over the scorching desert between the coastal mountains and the Andes, the fog **evaporates**.

 Stop here for the Strategy Break.

Strategy Break

If you were to create a problem-solution frame for this article so far, it might look like this:

What is the problem?

The people of Chungungo, Chile, had almost no fresh water.

Why is it a problem?

This made life harsh:
There were no gardens.
There were no trees.
Many people moved away.

Solutions

1. The people who stayed in Chungungo hired trucks to haul water from a well 25 miles away.

Results

1. They could only afford to use four gallons of water a day. Bathing in fresh water was a luxury.

As you read the rest of this article, pay attention to the other solutions that people try to solve the problem. When you finish reading, you will complete the problem-solution frame.

Go on reading.

Capturing Water

Scientists in Chile and Canada thought they could help the people of Chungungo. By studying a nearby grove of eucalyptus trees, they found a clue about how they might capture the fog's water.

On El Tofo, the tiny water droplets that make up the *camanchacas* collect on the trees' leaves, forming larger drops that fall to the ground. This grove seems to have constant rainfall from within. The scientists experimented to find a way of using this property of the fog to draw water out of it.

The basic idea was simple. They would place plastic nets upright, like sails, on the mountain. As the fog passed through the nets, many droplets would hit the netting, merge into larger drops, and run down toward the ground. At the bottom of the nets, the water could be collected.

To see if the idea would work, they placed small nets—one meter square—at various places along the mountain ridge of El Tofo. Some of these nets gathered several gallons of clean water per day. By noticing which nets collected the most water, scientists identified the best spots for placing larger nets.

The scientists helped the villagers put up seventy-five large nets, each about forty feet long and thirteen feet high. They built a system of gutters, pipes, and a reservoir to catch the water and make it flow to the village.

Would It Work?

At first, the villagers were **skeptical**. They never believed that water would flow to their homes. They joked that only fog or smoke would come out of the taps. But when the water flowed out of the pipes, the villagers were overjoyed. They had a party, dancing in the street and splashing one another with water.

Now water runs to every home in Chungungo. Small gardens bloom in most front yards, and meals in the village often include salads and vegetables.

Scientists say the system does not take vital water away from other areas. They estimate that the nets remove only one droplet from every one thousand water droplets in the fog—and all of that fog evaporates on the east side of the mountains anyway.

Many Dry Villages

Chungungo is not the only place with a water shortage. Since the success of the El Tofo project in 1992, the scientists have helped build similar systems in five other areas: one more in Chile, three in Peru, and one in Ecuador. A system for a second village in Ecuador is being built. And scientists have set up small nets to see if the idea will work in the African country of Namibia.

The effort to make rain where it is needed is as old as the human race. But the fog project in Chungungo is the first time that the results of trying to bring down water from the sky can be measured in gallons. ●

Strategy Follow-up

Now complete the problem-solution frame with information from the second part of this article.

What is the problem?

The people of Chungungo, Chile, had almost no fresh water.

Why is it a problem?

This made life harsh:
There were no gardens.
There were no trees.
Many people moved away.

Solutions	Results
1. The people who stayed in Chungungo hired trucks to haul water from a well twenty-five miles away.	**1.** They could only afford to use four gallons of water a day. Bathing in fresh water was a luxury.
2.	**2.**
3.	**3.** END RESULT:

✓Personal Checklist

Read each question and put a check (✓) in the correct box.

1. How well do you understand the information presented in this article?
   - ☐ 3 (extremely well)
   - ☐ 2 (fairly well)
   - ☐ 1 (not well)

2. In Building Background, how well were you able to list ways to solve the problem of very little rainfall?
   - ☐ 3 (extremely well)
   - ☐ 2 (fairly well)
   - ☐ 1 (not well)

3. How well were you able to complete the paragraph in the Vocabulary Builder?
   - ☐ 3 (extremely well)
   - ☐ 2 (fairly well)
   - ☐ 1 (not well)

4. How well were you able to complete the problem-solution frame in the Strategy Follow-up?
   - ☐ 3 (extremely well)
   - ☐ 2 (fairly well)
   - ☐ 1 (not well)

5. How well do you understand why the villagers of Chungungo were skeptical of the scientists' nets?
   - ☐ 3 (extremely well)
   - ☐ 2 (fairly well)
   - ☐ 1 (not well)

Vocabulary Check

Look back at the work you did in the Vocabulary Builder. Then answer each question by circling the correct letter.

1. What does the word *harsh* mean in the context of this selection?
   a. ugly
   b. rough
   c. loud

2. Which word is an antonym of *luxury*?
   a. hardship
   b. comfort
   c. treat

3. What is an example of something that evaporates?
   a. water freezing into ice
   b. water turning into steam
   c. ice melting into water

4. What does a person feel when he or she is skeptical?
   a. faith
   b. anger
   c. doubt

5. What do the people of Chile call the fogs that roll over the mountains?
   a. chungungos
   b. tofos
   c. *camanchacas*

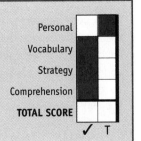

Add the numbers that you just checked to get your Personal Checklist score. Fill in your score here. Then turn to page 209 and transfer your score onto Graph 1.

Personal
Vocabulary
Strategy
Comprehension
TOTAL SCORE
✓ T

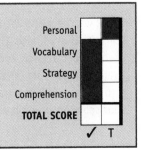

Check your answers with your teacher. Give yourself 1 point for each correct answer, and fill in your Vocabulary score here. Then turn to page 209 and transfer your score onto Graph 1.

Personal
Vocabulary
Strategy
Comprehension
TOTAL SCORE
✓ T

Strategy Check

Review the problem-solution frame that you completed in the Strategy Follow-up. Also review the article if necessary. Then answer these questions:

1. Which sentence does *not* describe a problem that the people of Chungungo faced?

    a. There were no gardens in Chungungo.

    b. The people had almost no fresh water.

    c. The people lived by fishing in the ocean.

2. What was the result of people hiring trucks to haul water to Chungungo?

    a. They could only afford to use four gallons of water a day.

    b. They could bathe in as much fresh water they wanted.

    c. Water flowed out of the pipes, and the villagers were overjoyed.

3. What did the scientists study in order to try and solve the water problem?

    a. They studied how people used their water.

    b. They studied life on El Tofo Mountain.

    c. They studied a grove of eucalyptus trees.

4. After the one-meter nets caught several gallons of water a day, what solution did the scientists try?

    a. hiring trucks to haul water from 25 miles away

    b. smaller nets and a system to make the water flow to the ocean

    c. larger nets and a system to make the water flow to the village

5. What is the end result of the villagers' problem?

    a. Water flows out of the pipes and into every home in Chungungo.

    b. Some of the one-meter nets gather several gallons of water a day.

    c. Fog and smoke come out of the taps and into every home in Chungungo.

Comprehension Check

Review the article if necessary. Then answer these questions:

1. Why was hauling water by truck not a very good solution to the problem?

    a. It was very expensive to haul the water.

    b. Each villager could only use four gallons a day.

    c. Both of the above answers are correct.

2. What did scientists learn from studying a grove of eucalyptus trees?

    a. They learned how the eucalyptus grew to be so tall.

    b. They found a clue about how to capture the fog's water.

    c. Neither of the above answers is correct.

3. How did the scientists know where to put the 75 large nets?

    a. They noticed which of the small nets collected the most water.

    b. They used a map and a computer to draw the mountain ridge.

    c. They flew over the area in a plane and looked for the wettest spots.

4. How many droplets do scientist estimate that the nets remove from the fog?

    a. one droplet from every one thousand

    b. one droplet from every ten thousand

    c. one droplet from every one million

5. Since building the water system in Chungungo, how many similar systems have scientists helped build?

    a. one

    b. three

    c. five

Check your answers with your teacher. Give yourself 1 point for each correct answer, and fill in your Strategy score here. Then turn to page 209 and transfer your score onto Graph 1.

Personal		
Vocabulary		
Strategy		
Comprehension		
TOTAL SCORE	✓	T

Check your answers with your teacher. Give yourself 1 point for each correct answer, and fill in your Comprehension score here. Then turn to page 209 and transfer your score onto Graph 1.

Personal		
Vocabulary		
Strategy		
Comprehension		
TOTAL SCORE	✓	T

Extending

Choose one or more of these activities:

CREATE A SCENE
Draw a mural or create a diorama that illustrates the problem in Chungungo and how it was solved.

STAGE A NEWS REPORT
Imagine that you are a reporter covering the events in Chungungo. Use the information from this article to write a script for a headline news report. Be sure to create an attention-grabbing headline.

LEARN MORE ABOUT DRY PLACES
Use the sources listed on this page to learn more about dry places around the world. Make a list of the problems that they face and some of the solutions that they have used to solve them.

Resources

Web Sites
http://www.fogquest.org/
This is a Web site for an organization that promotes the use of fog collectors and other water-collection methods in developing countries. Click on "Project Information" for descriptions of specific projects.

http://www.ucmp.berkeley.edu/glossary/gloss5/biome/deserts.html
This Web page describes the four major types of deserts around the world.

Learning New Words

From Lesson 17
• cell
• stylus

From Lesson 19
• animated

From Lesson 20
• harsh

Multiple-Meaning Words

As you know, a single word can have more than one meaning. For example, the word *cell* can mean "a small room," "the matter that living things are made of," or "a box-shaped arrangement of dots." To figure out which meaning of *cell* an author is using, you have to use context. Context is the information surrounding a word or situation that helps you understand it.

When you read "Louis Braille and His Dots" you used context clues to figure out that the meaning of *cell* in that selection was "box-shaped arrangement of dots." Now use context to figure out the correct meaning of each underlined word. Circle the letter of the correct meaning.

1. Jack was in the hospital because his white blood <u>cell</u> count was low.

   a.   the matter that living things are made of

   b.   small room in a prison or convent

2. Amy's phonograph was so old that they didn't make the <u>stylus</u> for it anymore.

   a.   small, pointed writing tool

   b.   needle of a record player

3. The comic strip was <u>animated</u> in a happy, cartoonish style.

   a.   full of life

   b.   drawn

4. The car's screeching brakes were very <u>harsh</u>.

   a.   unpleasing or jarring to the ear

   b.   rugged or bleak

5. Everyone gathered in the <u>square</u> to take part in the New Year's celebration.

   a.   figure or shape having four equal sides

   b.   space in a city surrounded by four streets

Antonyms

An antonym is a word that means the opposite of another word. The author of "The Mammoth" uses several antonym pairs, especially when describing the motion of the roller coaster. For example, The Mammoth moved *slowly* and *quickly* as it *rose* and *fell*.

Draw a line from each word in Column 1 to its antonym in Column 2.

Column 1	Column 2
forget	finish
start	dirty
inner	evening
rich	remember
morning	poor
clean	outer

Combining Forms

A combining form is a word part that is added to another word or combining form to make a new word. For example, you know that *ambi-* is a combining form. If you add it to the word *dexterity*, you create the word *ambidexterity*, which means "the ability to use both hands equally well."

mono-

The combining form *mono-* means "having one _____" or "one _____."
In Lesson 19 you learned that a *monologue* is a speech that is made by one person.

Complete each sentence with one of the words below. Use a dictionary if necessary.

monosyllabic   monogram   monoplane

1. An aircraft with one pair of wings is called a _____.

2. The words *you, me, they,* and *it* are all _____.

3. When a person's initials are combined to make one design, they form a

_____.

VOCABULARY

From Lesson 18
- above/below
- danger/safety
- day/night
- fell/rose
- quickly/slowly
- sick/well

From Lesson 19
- monologue

Graphing Your Progress

The graphs on page 209 will help you track your progress as you work through this book. Follow these directions to fill in the graphs:

Graph 1

1. Start by looking across the top of the graph for the number of the lesson you just finished.

2. In the first column for that lesson, write your Personal Checklist score in both the top and bottom boxes. (Notice the places where *13* is filled in on the sample.)

3. In the second column for that lesson, fill in your scores for the Vocabulary, Strategy, and Comprehension Checks.

4. Add the three scores, and write their total in the box above the letter *T*. (The *T* stands for "Total." The ✓ stands for "Personal Checklist.")

5. Compare your scores. Does your Personal Checklist score match or come close to your total scores for that lesson? Why or why not?

Graph 2

1. Again, start by looking across the top of the graph for the number of the lesson you just finished.

2. In the first column for that lesson, shade the number of squares that match your Personal Checklist score.

3. In the second column for that lesson, shade the number of squares that match your total score.

4. As you fill in this graph, you will be able to check your progress across the book. You'll be able to see your strengths and areas of improvement. You'll also be able to see areas where you might need a little extra help. You and your teacher can discuss ways to work on those areas.

Graph 1

For each lesson, enter the scores from your Personal Checklist and your Vocabulary, Strategy, and Comprehension Checks. Total your scores and then compare them. Does your Personal Checklist score match or come close to your total scores for that lesson? Why or why not?

Go down to Graph 2 and shade your scores for the lesson you just completed.

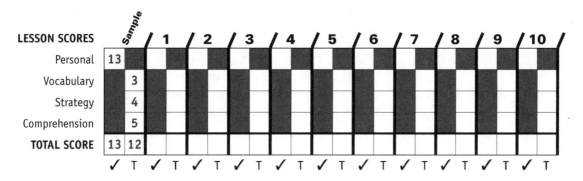

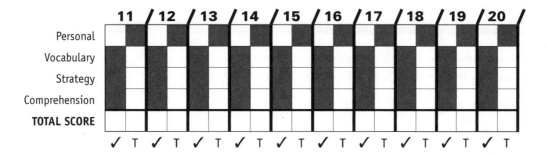

Graph 2

Now record your overall progress. In the first column for the lesson you just completed, shade the number of squares that match your Personal Checklist score. In the second column for that lesson, shade the number of squares that match your total score. As you fill in this graph, you will be able to check your progress across the book.

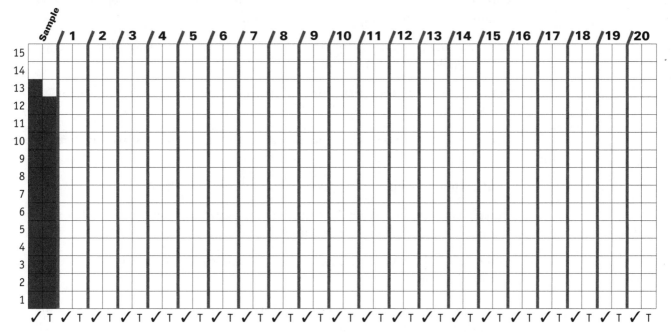

Glossary of Terms

This glossary includes definitions for important terms introduced in this book.

antonym   a word that means the opposite of another word. *Quickly* and *slowly* are antonyms of each other.

author's purpose   the reason or reasons that an author has for writing a particular selection. Authors write for one or more of these purposes: to *entertain* (make you laugh), to *inform* (explain or describe something), to *persuade* (try to get you to agree with their opinion), to *express* (share their feelings or ideas about something).

biography   the true story of a person's life, written by someone else.

cause-and-effect relationship   the relationship between events in a piece of writing. The cause in a cause-and-effect relationship tells *why* something happened; the effect tells *what* happened.

cause-and-effect chain   a graphic organizer used for recording the cause-and-effect relationships in a piece of writing.

characters   the people or animals that perform the action in a story.

character wheel   a graphic organizer used for recording the changes that a character goes through from the beginning to the end of a story.

combining form   a word part that is added to another word or combining form to make a new word. When the combining form *psycho-* is added to the word *therapy,* the word *psychotherapy* is formed.

comparing   looking at how two or more things are alike.

comparison chart   a graphic organizer used for showing how two or more people, places, things, or events are alike and different.

compound word   a word that is made up of two words put together. *Sundial* and *weekend* are examples of compound words.

concept map   a graphic organizer used for recording the main ideas and supporting details in a piece of writing.

conclusion   a decision that is reached after thinking about certain facts or information.

context   information that comes before and after a word or situation to help you understand it.

contrasting   looking at how two or more things are different.

description   in nonfiction, the organizational pattern that explains what something is, what it does, or how and why it works.

end result   the solution a character or characters try that finally solves the problem in a story.

event   a happening. The plot of any story contains one or more events during which the characters try to solve their problems.

fiction stories about made-up characters or events. Forms of fiction include short stories, historical fiction, fantasy, and folktales.

first-person point of view the perspective, or viewpoint, of one of the characters in a story. That character uses words such as *I, me, my,* and *mine* to tell the story.

graphic organizer a chart, graph, or drawing used to show how the main ideas in a piece of writing are organized and related.

headings the short titles given throughout a piece of nonfiction. The headings often state the main ideas of a selection.

informational article a piece of writing that gives facts and details about a particular subject, or topic.

main idea the most important idea of a paragraph, section, or whole piece of writing.

multiple-meaning word a word that has more than one meaning. The word *cell* is a multiple-meaning word whose meanings include "a small room," "the matter that living things are made of," and "a box-shaped arrangement of dots."

myth a story that usually explains something in nature, such as why there are solar eclipses or why elephants have trunks.

narrator the person or character who is telling a story.

nonfiction writing that gives facts and information about real people, events, and topics. Informational articles and biographies are some forms of nonfiction.

organizational pattern in nonfiction, the pattern in which the text is written and organized. Common organizational patterns include description, cause-effect, sequence, compare-contrast, and problem-solution.

outline a framework for organizing the main ideas and supporting details in a piece of writing. Some outlines are organized according to a system of Roman numerals (I, II, III, IV, V, and so on), capital letters (A, B, C, D, E, and so on), and Arabic numerals (1, 2, 3, 4, 5, and so on).

plot the sequence of events in a piece of writing.

point of view the perspective, or viewpoint, from which a story is told.

prediction a kind of guess that is based on the context clues given in a story.

problem difficulty or question that a character must solve or answer.

problem-solution frame a graphic organizer used for recording the problem, solutions, and end result in a piece of writing.

sequence the order of events in a piece of writing. The sequence shows what happens or what to do first, second, and so on.

sequence chain a graphic organizer used for recording the sequence of events in a piece of writing. Sequence chains are used mostly for shorter periods of time, and time lines are used mostly for longer periods of time.

setting the time and place in which a story happens.

signal words words and phrases that tell when something happens or when to do something. Examples of signal words are *first, next, finally, after lunch, two years later,* and *in 1820.*

solution   the things that characters or people do to solve a problem.

specialized vocabulary   words that are related to a particular subject, or topic. Specialized vocabulary words in the selection "Bears" include *habitats, hibernating,* and *prey.*

story map   a graphic organizer used for recording the main parts of a story: its title, setting, character, problem, events, and solution.

suffix   a word part that is added to the end of a word. Adding a suffix usually changes the word's meaning and function. For example, the suffix *-less* means "without," so the word *painless* changes from the noun *pain* to an adjective meaning "without pain."

summary   a short description. A summary describes what has happened so far in a piece of fiction, or what the main ideas are in a piece of nonfiction.

supporting details   details that describe or explain the main idea of a paragraph, section, or whole piece of text.

synonym   a word that has the same meaning as another word. *Fast* and *quick* are synonyms of each other.

third-person point of view   the perspective, or viewpoint, of a narrator who is not a character in a story. That narrator uses words such as *she, her, he, his, they,* and *their* to tell the story.

time line   a graphic organizer used for recording the sequence of events in a piece of writing. Time lines are used mostly for longer periods of time, and sequence chains are used mostly for shorter periods of time.

title   the name of a piece of writing.

topic   the subject of a piece of writing. The topic is what the selection is all about.

Acknowledgments

Acknowledgment is gratefully made to the following publishers, authors, and agents for permission to reprint these works. Every effort has been made to determine copyright owners. In the case of any omissions, the Publisher will be pleased to make suitable acknowledgments in future editions.

"Arachne the Spinner" retold by Geraldine McCaughrean. Reprinted with the permission of Margaret K. McElderry Books, an imprint of Simon & Schuster Children's Publishing Division from Greek Myths by Geraldine McCaughrean. Text copyright © 1992 Geraldine McCaughrean. Also from *The Orchard Book of Greek Myths* by Geraldine McCaughrean. First published in the UK by Orchard Books in 1992, a division of The Watts Publishing Group Limited, 96 Leonard Street, London EC2A 4XD. Reprinted by permission of The Watts Publishing Group Limited.

"Bears" by Dorothy Hinshaw Patent as appeared in *Spider,* August 1995. Reprinted by permission of the author.

"Five Words!" by Pnina Kass as appeared in *Cricket,* September 1991, Vol. 19, No. 1. Reprinted by permission of the author.

"A Greenland Rope Trick" by K. C. Tessendorf. Reprinted by permission of *Cricket* magazine, January 1998, Vol. 25, No. 5. Copyright © 1998 by K. C. Tessendorf.

"Learning To Disobey" by Margery Facklam from *What Does the Crow Know? The Mysteries of Animal Intelligence.* Text copyright © 1994 by Margery Facklam. Reprinted by permission of Sierra Club Books for Children.

"Lefthanders in a Righthanded World" by Dr. Alvin Silverstein and Virginia B. Silverstein from *The Lefthander's World.* Copyright © 1997 by Alvin and Virginia Silverstein. Reprinted by permission of the authors.

"Louis Braille and His Dots" by Paulette Bochnig Sharkey. Reprinted by permission of *Spider* magazine, April 1997, Vol. 4, No. 4. Copyright © 1997 by Paulette Bochnig Sharkey.

"The Mammoth" by Michele G. Bonnee. From *Child Life,* copyright © 1987 by Children's Better Health Institute, Benjamin Franklin Literary & Medical Society, Inc., Indianapolis, Indiana. Used by permission.

"A Mare Called Lucky" by H. J. Hutchins. Reprinted by permission of *Cricket* magazine, March 1998, Vol. 25, No. 7. Copyright © 1994 by H. J. Hutchins.

"Mayday!" by Redvers Brandling from *The Young Oxford Book of Ghost Stories.* Reprinted by permission of the author.

"Mother and Daughter" from *Baseball in April and Other Stories.* Copyright © 1990 by Gary Soto. Reprinted by permission of Harcourt, Inc.

"The Mysterious Treasure of Oak Island" by Seymour Simon from *Strange Mysteries from Around the World.* (Four Wind Press, 1980).

"The Parcel Post Kid" by Michael O. Tunnell. Reprinted by permission of *Spider* magazine, July 1997, Vol. 4, No. 7. Copyright © 1997 by Michael O. Tunnell.